L
THE BIBLE
SPEAK

By
Ali Muhsin

Islamic Book Service

LET THE BIBLE SPEAK
By Ali Muhsin

ISBN: 81-7231-496-5

Edition- 2003

Published by *Abdul Naeem* for
Islamic Book Service
2241, Kucha Chelan, Darya Ganj, New Delhi-110 002
Ph.: 23253514, 23265380, 23286551, Fax: 23277913
E-mail: ibsdelhi@del2.vsnl.net.in
    ibsdelhi@mantraonline.com
    islamic@eth.net
website: http//www.islamic-india.com

Published with the permission of
ISLAMIC DA'WAH AND GUIDANCE CENTER
Dammam - Postal Code 31131 - K.S.A.
Ph.: 8263535 - 8272772

Printed at: *Noida Printing Press,* C-31, Sector-7, Noida (Ghaziabad) U.P.

CONTENTS

FOREWORD

Being totally convinced that this book (Let the Bible Speak) contains good information about The Bible and The Holy Qur'ân, The Dammam Islamic Da'wah and Guidance Center decided to reprint it again. But as we prepare to do the job we have noticed that the copy that was available was too blurred and not good enough for reproduction.

Due to this problem, Dammam Da'wah Guidance Center work it out to review, retyped, annotates and corrects the whole book, such as;

1. Some references are missing.

2. Some quotation

3. Misspelling

4. Typing errors

5. Some chapters and verses are not accurate

We have tried our utmost to reproduce the book as it is with some minute changes to ensure that the book will not lose its internal beauty for the benefit of all who read it.

To the author, Ali Muhsin, We pray that the Almighty Allâh continuously showers His Mercy and Grace to him and add the virtue of this book to his scale of good deeds.

We ask Allâh's pardon for any mistake that we commit unknowingly, as it has been for us in preparing it.

Islamic Da'wah and Guidance Center
Dammam - Postal Code 31131 - K.S.A.
Tel.: 8263535 - 8272772

(Ramadan 1415)

ACKNOWLEDGEMENT

My thanks are due to Kingsley Green, an Australian biology teacher in the Mazengo Secondary School, Dodoma, Tanzania, who as a lay preacher used to pay us visits in prison. From him I learn to study the Bible systematically.

To the many Christian preachers at College and in prison, fellow students and fellow inmates, with whom I used to have fruitful discussions I owe gratitude.

I would also like to express thanks to the Amnesty International for keeping me supplied with reading matter which enlarged my knowledge of present-day Chrsitian thinking.

To Zainab Sabri, daughter of a very good Egyptian friend of mine, Mr. Fathi Sabri, I must say: Thank you ! for typing the first manuscript.

To my dear wife, Azza, I am indebted for her courage to sustain difficulties and for the peace of mind which she gave me and which enabled me in prison to study, to meditate, and to write all that I have written. On her lonely shoulders rested the burden of looking after herself and our six children for ten long years while she was living as a refugee in Egypt.

Over and above all I thank Allâh who has guided me along the right path.

PREFACE

The writing and publication of this essay is not intended to be an exercise in polemics. Rather is it motivated by the desire to enlighten both Chrisitans and Muslims who in many parts of the world have to live together as fellow countrymen and neighbours. Their enlightenment regarding the original fundamentals of each other's faith would, it is hoped, make them appreciate the basic unity that binds them as adherents of the same original faith, the Universal Religion which teaches submission to the will of the one True God as the basis on which man's moral behaviour is founded.

It is unfortunate that Jesus Christ has left for us nothing as authoritative as the Prophet Muhammad has done. In the Qur'ân are the teachings of Islam in their unsullied purity. We do not find the same in the Gospels (Injeel). The latter may be compared to the traditions of the Prophet (the Hadiths or Sunnah). Of the sayings and the actions of Jesus as reported in the Bible there are admittedly many which are spurious, false, just as there were established and the weak and false were weeded out. It is undeniable that attempts were made, for sectarian and other divisive reasons, to fake sayings and attribute them to the Prophet.

Impartial criticism would have to admit, however, that there was much more scientific methodology when the Prophet's traditions came to be collected and shifted than there has been at the adoption of the canonical Gospels. The great scholars (Imams) who devoted their lives collecting the traditions of the Prophet made their best endeavors (Ijtihad) using strictly scienctific standards to verify the genuine traditions. But even their best endeavors and their scientific methods were after all human and not infallible. Fortunately there is the Qur'ân whose authenticity has never been questioned by friend or foe. That is the unshakable foundation of Islam on which the tenets of the faith are based. It is the final criterion of the genuineness of any tradition, and the rock on which the structure of Islam has been built.

In the following pages it will be seen that I have tended to reproduce many quotations. This is my way of dealing with the subject seriously, particularly a subject of such transcendent importance as religion. I do not want to be among *"Those who would argue about God without knowledge, and without guidance and without an enlightening book,"* as the Qur'ân puts it.

Studying the Bible in the long solitude of my prison cell I attempted to search for the true teachings of Jesus and the Hebrew Prophets who had preceded him. Ten years and five months of imprisonment became ten years and five months of intensive Bible study. Painstakingly I kept removing bit by bit the hard encrustation which had piled up on what I knew must be a lustrous lying beneath.

I found it.

I would appeal to both my Muslim brothers and sisters who know very little of Christianity, and to my Christian friends who know next to nothing about true Islam (and true Christianity for that matter) to come along with me, and in the following pages search for the truth. We will find it, for the truth is the house that has been founded upon the Rock, and rain shall fall, and the winds shall blow, but the house shall not fall. There in Holy Jerusalem whence both Muhammad and Jesus rose in spiritual ecstasy to the Heavenly Presence is a symbol of glaring significance, denoting the truth that bids both Muslim and Christian bow to the same God who is worshipped with equal fervor and devotion in the Mosque upon the Rock and in the Church of the Holy Sepulchre. That Truth bids us rid ourselves of the traditions of men and follow the commandments of God. That Truth bids us relinquish the tendency to divide Religion into sects and uphold the Unity that binds us together.

Allâh says in the Holy Qur'ân:

"And We verily gave Moses the Scripture, that haply they might go aright. And We made the son of Mary and his mother a portent, and We gave them a refuge on a height, a place of flocks and water-springs. O ye Messengers! Eat of the good things, and to right. Lo! I am aware of what ye do. And lo! this your religion is one religion and I am your Lord, so keep your duty unto Me. But they (mankind) have broken their religion among them into sects, each sect rejoicing in its tenets. So leave them in their error till a time."

Qur'ân 23:49-54

Let us not keep on wandering in error when the Straight Path is clear before us. Let us understand one another and appreciate one another's honesty in seeking for the truth.

Ali Muhsin

"PIETY BASED ON ERROR IS INDEFENSIBLE"

Father John L. Mackenzie

THE TEACHING OF THE CHURCH

By the term "the church" is meant the body of Christians, or more precisely, the professional priesthood which has taken upon itself the task of formulating doctrines and rituals as well as rendering certain religious services in accordance with what are believed to be the teachings of Jesus Christ. "The church" may also mean the sect to which an individual Christian belongs.

All the main Christian Churches, or sects, teach the following as the principal dogmas, or articles of faith to be believed in without question:

1. There is One God.

2. In God there are three divine Persons, the Father, the Son and the Holy Ghost, Holy Spirit. These three Persons are called the blessed Trinity. They are equal and they are eternal i.e. they have no beginning and no end. They are not three gods, but One God.

3. The Father is God and the first Person of the blessed Trinity.

4. The Son is God and the second Person of the Trinity. He is Jesus Christ who is God who took the human form. He was born of the Virgin Mary about two thousand years ago in Palestine, was crucified, died and rose again from the dead. His death and suffering on the cross was intended to be a sacrifice for the forgiveness of the sins of men. This is called the Atonement, and he is entitled the Savior and the Redeemer.

5. The Holy Spirit is the third Person of the blessed Trinity. After the death of Christ the Holy Spirit descended upon the Apostles (or early Missionaries) of Christ, and the

Spirit continues to lead the Church.

6. Every human child bears with him the stain of what is called the "Original Sin" inherited from the transgression of Adam.

7. BAPTISM, the ceremony of sprinkling somebody with water, or, according to some sects, immersing him in water, as making his being accepted as a member of the Church, and belief in Christ's atonement is the only means whereby man shall be saved.

Let us examine the sacred doctrines of the Church in the light of the writings of the Bible which the Church accepts a canonical, that is to say, as the authoritative Word of God.

THE BIBLE

The word Bible comes from the Greek **biblia** meaning "books". It is a collection of many books which form the foundation of Christian belief. Admittedly they have been written by a large number of authors, known and unknown. But those authors are believed to have been inspired by God and they wrote the books under the supervision and guidance of God; hence the Bible is referred to as The Word of God. The Catholic Bible, however, is somewhat different from the Protestant Bible. The former consist of 73 books, while the latter has only 66 books.

In general the Bible is divided into two main portions, The Old Testament which was written before the advent of Jesus Christ, and the New Testament which was written after Jesus Christ and describes the life and teachings of Jesus Christ and the activities of his disciples, or apostles, in spreading the Christian faith. The New Testament contains also letters addressed to various Christian groups and individuals. These letters were written mostly by Paul, a Jew who converted to Christianity and became the chief exponents of the Christian faith as it is known today. He has at times described the true founder of modern Christianity.

The books of the Old Testament in their present form were probably written after the return of the Jews from the Babylonian captivity i.e. after 536 B.C. Those of the New Testament were collected and accepted as legal in the fourth century after Christ (about 367 A.D.) Besides the Four Gospels (describing the life and teaching of Christ) which are in the Bible there are a number of other Gospels which were not accepted by the Church elders, and some of them are available even today. The books which could have formed part of the Bible, and indeed were and are accepted by some Christians, but which the main body of the Christian Church rejected, are called the **Apocrypha**, a Greek word meaning "Hidden". But which now has wrongly been understood as meaning **"false, not genuine"**. The officially accepted books are called "Canonical". It is these canonical books of the Bible which are regarded as THE WORD OF GOD.

ORIGINAL SIN

In the Old Testament the first book, Genesis, has the story of creation and the fall of man. Thus is described the fall of Adam from grace.

"The Lord God took the man and put him in the garden of Eden to till it and keep it. And the Lord God commanded the man, Saying, "You may freely eat of every tree of the garden; but of the tree of knowledge of good and evil you shall not eat, for in the day that you eat of it you shall die."
Genesis 2:15-16

Adam, however, persuaded by his wife, Eve, transgressed God's command and ate of the forbidden tree of knowledge. God cursed them both.

To the woman He said; *"I will greatly multiply your pain in childbearing; in pain you shall bring forth children, yet your desire shall be for your husband, and he shall rule over you."*

3

And to Adam He said; *"Because you have listened to the voice of your wife, and have eaten of the tree of which I commanded you, "you shall not eat of it", cursed is the ground because of you; in toil you shall eat of it all the days of your life; thorns and thistles it shall bring forth to you; and you shall eat the plants of the field. In the sweat of your face you shall eat bread till you return to the ground, for out of it you were taken; you are dust, and to dust you shall return."* Genesis 3:16-19

On account of their sin, the Church teaches, Adam and Eve lost sanctifying grace, the right of Heaven and their special gifts, they became subject to death, to suffering and to a strong inclination to evil and they were driven from the garden of Paradise. On account of Adam's sin all human beings are born deprived of sanctifying grace and inherit his punishment. This is what is called **THE ORIGINAL SIN**.

St. Paul's theology developed the doctrine of Original Sin to justify another doctrine, **REDEMPTION** by the death of Jesus on the cross. In his letter to the Romans he wrote:

"Therefore as sin came into the world through one man and death through sin, and so death spread to all men because all men sinned - sin indeed was in the world before the law was given, but sin is not counted where there is no law. Yet death reigned from Adam to Moses, even over those whose sins were not like the transgression of Adam, who was a type of the one who was to come. But the free gift is not like the trespass. For if many died through one man's trespass, much more have the grace of God and the free gift in the grace of that one man Jesus Christ abounded for many." Romans 5:12-15

To the Corinthians St. Paul wrote: *"For as in Adam all die, so also in Christ shall all be made alive."*

1 Corinthians 15:22

The Pauline doctrine of Original Sin is, however, contradicted by other passages from the Bible. In Deuteronomy, for example, which is one of the five books of Torah, *Moses says: "The fathers shall not be put to death for the children, nor shall the children be put to death for the fathers; every man shall be put to death for his own sin."*

Deuteronomy 24:16

In Jeremiah we read: "In those days they shall no longer say; "The fathers have eaten sour grapes, and the children's teeth are set on edge." But every one shall die for his own sin; each man who eats sour grapes, his teeth shall be set on edge."   *Jeremiah 31:29-30*

And in Ezekiel it is more categorically stated:

"Yet you say, Why should not the son suffer for the iniquity of the father? When the son has done what is lawful and right, and has been careful to observe all my statutes, he shall not suffer for the iniquity of the father, nor the father suffer for the iniquity of the son; the righteousness of the righteous shall be upon himself, and the wickedness of the wicked shall be upon himself."

Ezekiel 18:19-20

In the New Testament too there is the evidence of Jesus himself contradicting the theory of inherited sin:

"As he passed by, he (Jesus) saw a man blind from his birth, and his disciples asked, "Rabbi, who sinned, this man or his parents, that he was born blind?" Jesus answered, "It was not this man sinned, or his parents, but that the works of God might be made manifest in him."   *John 9:1-3*

Contrary to the teachings of the Church, which goes under his name, that all children are born in sin, **Jesus Christ confirms their innocence in the following passage from the Gospel according to Matthew:**

5

"Truly, I say to you, unless you turn and become like children you will never enter the kingdom of heaven."

Matthew 18:3

Thus we see that the doctrine of inherited sin propounded by Paul as in his first letter to the Corinthians (quoted above) is contradicted by God and Moses in more authoritative evidence from the Bible, namely in Deuteronomy, Jeremiah and Ezekiel (all of the Old Testament) as well as by Jesus Christ in the Gospels according to John and Matthew (in the New Testament). The Church however is inclined to disregard the categorical evidence of the Torah, the Prophets and the Gospels, which form the main parts of the Bible, and rely on the letters of St. Paul which for no earthly reason were appended to and then incorporated in the Bible.

But who is this Paul:

ST. PAUL

St. Paul was a Jew who was born in Tarsus in what is now Turkey. When he was born the country was part of Roman Empire, and thus although by race and religion a Jew, he yet enjoyed the privilege of being a Roman citizen. St. Paul was not one of the disciples chosen by Jesus in his life-time. Indeed there is no indication that he ever met Jesus. What is known is that he was fanatical in hatred for Christians, and engaged himself in hounding out Christians from hiding and bringing them to be tortured and killed. He was present at the stoning of St. Stephen, the first Christian martyr.

While on his way to Damascus he is reported to have experienced a vision of Christ, and thus became a staunch propagator of Christianity which he claimed had been revealed to him by Jesus in visions. This "revealed" version of Christianity was fundamentally different from what the chosen disciples of Jesus knew to be the teaching of the Master, so that there was a serious conflict between Paul and the original followers of Christ who like Jesus had never deviated from the law of Moses and the strict Judaic monotheism.

THE ONLY SON OF GOD

In the four Gospels of the Bible there are a number of references to Jesus Christ as the "Son of God". The following are a few examples.

"And when the centurion, who stood facing him, saw that he thus breathed his last, he said, "truly this man was the Son of God!"
Mark 15:39

And the angel said to her, "The Holy Spirit will come upon you, and the power of the Most High will overshadow you; therefore the child to be born will be called holy, the Son of God."   *Luke 1:35*

And they all said, "Are you the Son of God, then?" and he said to them, You say that I am."   *Luke 22:70*

He trust in God; let God deliver him now, If he desires; for he said, "I am the Son of God."   *Matthew 27:43*

And whenever the unclean spirits beheld him, they fell down before him and cried out, "You are the Son of God." And he strictly ordered them not to make him known.

Mark 3:11-12

And when he came to the other side, to the country of Gadarenes, two demoniac met him, coming out of the tombs, so fierce that no one could pass that way. And behold, they cried out, What have you to do with us, O Son of God? Have you come here to torment us before the time?"

Matthew 8:28-29

In the Gospels of Matthew, Mark and Luke there are about 22 such references to Jesus as the Son of God,

but in all of them not once did he call himself so.
Matthew 27:43 Quoted above refers to the allegation of the
chief priest with the scribes and the elders who mocked him.
It was not first hand reporting of Jesus's own statement by
the author of the Gospel. It was normally either madmen, the
so called demoniac and unclean spirits, or pagan Roman soldiers
who referred to him as the Son of God. **His own preference
was for the title of Ben Adam**, which just meant man or
son of man. **That title is repeated about 80 times in the
Gospels.** His Jewish persecutors out of malice alleged that
he claimed to be King of the Jews that he might incur the wrath
of the Roman rulers, and that he claimed to be the Son of
God to enrage the Jewish people.

Francis Young, Lecturer in the New Testament Studies
at Birmingham University, writing in The **Myth of God Incarnate**
says: *"Apart from John where interpretive material is
clearly placed upon the lips of Jesus, the Gospels invariably
portray not Jesus but others as using phrases like the
"Holy One of God", or "Son of David", or Son of God".
Alone of all the titles "Son of Man" regularly appears
as used by Jesus himself..."*

It should be remembered that at the time of Jesus it was
commonplace to invest with divinity not only non-existent
mythological figures but historian mortals as well. Laertus,
the pagan Author of the Lives of the Philosophers, writes of
a number of philosophers as being sons of God. **Plato** was
described as being of divine parentage; and so was **Pythagoras**
who was supposed to be the incarnate son of the god Hermes.
Empedocles was also alleged to be an immortal god who healed
the sick, and his followers worshipped him and prayed to him.
Plutarch regards it as beyond that **Alexander the Great** was
of divine descent and **Romulus** the legendary ancestor of the
Romans was the Son of Mars, the god of war. He was supposed
to have been raised to heaven in a cloud. An inscription of
48 B.C. refers to **Julius Caesar** as "god manifest offspring

of Ares and Aphrodite and common savior of human life". Another inscription referring to **Augustus Caesars** says: "The Emperor Caesar, Son of God, god Augustus, overseer of land and sea."

These titles of "god", "son of god" and "lord" being common and widespread in the Mediterranean region about the time of Jesus could not but influence the general public who were not deeply infused with the Judaic monotheism. They were terms loosely used by all and sundry.

The myths around those other personalities, mythological and historical, were strikingly similar to those later adopted by Christians in the case of the Prophet Jesus, on whom be peace. Francis Young in his essay. ***Two Roots or a Tangled Mass***? writes inter alia:

"Moreover, one cannot dismiss out of hand the view that something of the same kind happened in the case of Jesus. There are, to take but one example, general similarities between Livy's account of Romulus and some synoptic narratives about Jesus: a virgin birth, conception by a god, a remarkable career, no trace of his remains after death, an appearance after death to commission his successors, the offering of prayers to him. It would be impossible to make a convincing case for direct influence; but people living at roughly the same time do seem to have produced mythological accounts with parallel motifs."

To return to the text of the Bible, when Jesus was brought before the court he refused to concur to the charge that he claimed to be the Son of God as madmen and pagans had been propagating about him: And the high priest stood up and said:

"Have you no answer to make? What is it that these men testify against you?" But Jesus was silent. And the high priest said to him, "I adjure you by the living God, tell us if you are the Christ, the Son of God." Jesus said to him. "You have said so. But I tell you hereafter you will see the son of man seated at the right hand of Power,

9

and coming on the clouds of heaven."   Matthew 26:62-64

The three Gospels of Matthew, Mark and Luke (called "synoptic" meaning common view because they agree in form and content) do not refer to Jesus as the "only" Son of God. It is the Gospel of John which lays special stress on the divinity of Jesus, and calls him, the Only Son of God.

"And the Word became flesh and dwelt among us, full of grace and truth; we have beheld his glory, glory as of the only Son from the Father."   John 1:14

"For God so loved the world that he gave his only Son, that whoever believes in him should not perish but have eternal life."   John 3:16

What is special about the use of the term "Son of God"? Going through the Bible we find such terms being used in reference to many others besides Jesus Christ. In the Old Testament, all of it having been written before the birth of Jesus we find the following examples:

"When men began to multiply on the face of the ground and daughters were born to them, the sons of God saw that the daughters of men were fair; and they took wives such of them as they chose."   Genesis 6:1-2

"On what were its bases sunk, or who laid its cornerstone, when the morning stars sang together, and all the sons of God shouted for joy?"   Job 38:6-7

"Yet the number of the people of Israel shall be like the sand of the sea, which can be neither measured nor numbered, and in the place where it was said to them, "You are not my people." It shall be said to them "Sons of the living God."   Hosea 1:10

Apparently it was quite common practice before the time of Jesus even for Hebrew writers on religious subjects to use the term "sons of God" in reference to those who were beloved of God. An Italian Biblical authority, Marcello Craveri, who

10

wrote *__The Life of Jesus__*, however, believes that the term has in history undergone changes through mistranslation. He writes:

"Actually, the Old Testament does contain the phrase *__ebed Yahweh__*, which, however, means "the servant of God", "the slave of God", God's liege subject. The Greek text of Septuagint translates it equivocally as *__(pais Theou)__*, in as much as *__pais__*, like the Latin *__puer__*, can mean either "little boy" or "slave", subsequently, it was quite simple to replace *__pais__* in the sense of "boy" with *__(hyos)__*, which means "son".

Indeed in Hebrew literature even the term "god" seems to have been rather loosely used. In Exodus we read of God addressing Moses and telling him about the relation which would be between him and Aaron:

"He shall speak for you to the people; and he shall be a mouth for you, and you shall be to him as God."

Exodus 4:16

Note again:

"I say, "You are gods, sons of the Most High, all of you nevertheless, you shall die like men and fall like any prince."
Psalm 82: 6-7

All those quotations are from the Old Testament. Let us now see what the New Testament has to say. Luke reports Jesus preaching.

"But love your enemies, and do good, and lend, expecting nothing in return; and your reward will be great, and you will be sons of the most High; for he is kind to the ungrateful and the selfish."
Luke 6:35

In the Gospel according to Matthew Jesus is reported to say:

"Blessed are the peacemakers for they shall be called sons of God."
Matthew 5:9

Paul in his letter to the Romans writes:

11

"For all who are led by the Spirit of God are sons of God."

Romans 8:14

The two men who are said to have done their utmost to ascribe divinity to Jesus Christ are John and Paul; and yet from the above quotation Paul definitely admits that Jesus was not the only son of God, but *"all who are led by the Spirit of God are sons of God."*

Let us see what John has to say, he who has coined the phrase, *"the only son of God"*. In the course of an argument Jesus had with the Jews who wanted to stone him, he asked of them for which of the good works that he had shown them were they stoning him?

The Jews answered him, "We stone you for no good works but for blasphemy; because you being a man, make yourself God." Jesus answered them, "Is it not written in your law, I said, you are gods! If he called them gods to whom the word of God came (and the scripture cannot be broken), do you say of him of whom the Father consecrated and sent into the world, "You are blaspheming" because I said "I am the son of God?"   *John 10:33-36*

In other words Jesus was pointing out to his Jewish persecutors that the term Son of God was no more blasphemous than the term *"gods"* which had been used in respect of others previous to him. At least that is what the writer of John's Gospel implies. Jesus's own personal preference was for the term *"son of man"*, in Hebrew, Arabic and Swahili: *"Ben Adam"*, which just means "man". This is repeated no less than 80 times in the New Testament, mostly spoken by Jesus himself. Not once is he reported to categorically call himself the Son of God in any special sense.

Finally let us consider Christ's last words when he was about to ascend to heaven as related in the Gospel of John:

"I am ascending to my Father and your Father, to

12

It is very clear to understand what Jesus meant by this single sentence, that his sonship was in no way different from the sonship of all men.

The American writer, Upton Sinclair, says in his book, *"A Personal Jesus"*: "And lest anyone think that: in calling God his Father he was proclaiming himself the Son, let it be made clear that he called God your Father, too. He said it eighteen times in the New Testament: "Your Heavenly Father Knoweth", and so on. He meant that we were all sons of God, and he was one of them."

GOD AND JESUS (Are they one and the same?)

Christian Churches teach that Jesus Christ is not only the Son of God, but that "he is very God". The Father, The Son and the Holy Spirit are one. Three in one, and one in Three. They are co-eternal and co-equal. Jesus is God, and God is Jesus. That is the Christian dogma, to which the majority of those who call themselves Christian subscribe.

St. Paul in his first letter to the Corinthians wrote:

"We are even found to be misrepresenting God, because we testified of God that <u>he raised Christ</u>, whom he did not raise if it is true that the dead are not raised."

1 Corinthians 15:15

In spite of Paul's alleged belief that Christ was the same being as God, he could not but say: "God Raised Christ". If Jesus and God were one and the same would it not have been more appropriate to speak of the operation in the following terms: Christ raised himself? If God raised Christ, the two could not possibly be the same being. One was definitely the performer and the other upon whom the operation was performed.

John, the other strong advocate of the divinity of Christ,

13

reports in his Gospel that Jesus said: "Let not your hearts be troubled; believe in God, believe also in me." The word "also" emphasize the distinction between God and Christ.

In the Acts of the Apostles we read: ***"And he (Stephen) said, "Behold, I see the heavens opened and the Son of man standing at the right hand of God."*** Acts 7:56

The Son of man, as Jesus preferred to call himself, is seen by Stephen to be standing at the right hand of God. Hence he cannot at the same time be God; and this is a description of a situation in heaven, He is no longer the Jesus of this world described in Hebrew 2 as having been "made like his brethren in every respect, so that he might become a merciful and faithful high priest in the service of God".

On the Mount of Olives to which Jesus fled hunted by the Jews, he took occasion to withdraw from his disciples, and there in seclusion prayed to God:

"Father, if thou art willing, remove this cup from me; nevertheless not my will, but thine be done." And there appeared to him an angel from heaven, strengthening him."

Luke 22:42-43

We note here three important things:

1. Jesus prays to God, Jesus worships God. Hence they are two separate beings of unequal status to the extent that one has to pray to the other.

2. They have two separate wills, but the will of Jesus, the son of man, is subordinate to that of God. God's will must prevail.

3. Jesus, being man, loses heart and weakens, and God Almighty, as the source of all strength, sends an angel to strengthen Jesus.

In the Gospel of John, Jesus says categorically:

"For the Father is Greater than I" John 14:28

14

And finally on the cross: *"And about the ninth hour Jesus cried with a loud voice, "Eli, Eli, la ma sabach-thani?", that is, "My God, my God, why hast thou forsaken me?""*

Matthew 27:46

It is clear from the above quotation that Jesus and God are not only separate entities but their will are different and could be even contradictory; the superior will must however prevail. What is shocking, however, is the despairing tone of Christ's supplication on the cross. Far from being the only begotten Son of God or God, we could not expect such weakness even from an ordinary mortal with a trust in God.

MIRACLES: But in whose Authority?

Among the proofs advanced by some to subtantiate the divinity of Jesus are the miracles which he is reputed by the Gospels to have performed. Examples of such miracles are the turning of water into wine, the healing of the leprous and the paralytic, the exorcising of the possessed, the raising of the dead, and walking on water. But the very same Gospels tell us that Jesus attributed all those miracles and everything that he ever did to the God who had sent him. Hence are a few examples.

"For I have not spoken on my own authority; the Father who sent me has himself given me commandment what to say and what to speak. And I know that his commandment is eternal life. I say, therefore, I say as the Father has bidden me." John 12:49-50

"I can do nothing on my own authority; as I hear, I judge; and my judgement is just, because I seek not my own will but the will of him who sent me." John 5:30

Jesus takes justifiable pride in speaking and acting on God's authority and in obedience to his command. In the story of the raising of Luzarus from the dead as related by John we read:

"Then Jesus, deeply moved again, came to the tomb; It was a cave, and a stone lay upon it. Jesus said, "Take away the stone". Martha, the sister of the dead man, said to him, "Lord, by this time there will be an odor, for he has been dead four days. "Jesus said to her, "Did I not tell you that if you would believe you would see the glory of God?" So they took away the stone. And Jesus lifted up his eyes and said, "Father, I thank thee that thou hearest me always, but I have said this on account of the people standing by, that they may believe that thou didst hear me."   *John 11:38-44*

From the above we note three things.

1. Jesus tell Martha that she "would see the glory of God," and not Jesus own glory, for Jesus always seeks the glory of God who sent him.

2. Jesus prays to God for miracle, and dutifully thanks God for answering his prayers.

3. Jesus takes pains to convince the spectators that it is indeed God who has sent him, and that what he does with God's authority.

Much is also made of Jesus's own rising from the dead, the so called resurrection. But all references to the event in the Bible make clear that it was God who raised him. He did not rise of his own volition. Indeed neither was he unique in the act.

In 2 Kings 4:32-35 we read of a child who was raised from the dead. Another case is reported in 1 Kings 17:22. The Bible also tells of people who went up to heaven.

"And as they still went on and talked, behold, a chariot of fire and horses of fire separated the two of them. And Elija went up by a whirlwind into heaven."

2 Kings 2:11

"Enoch walked with God: and he was not, for God took him."

Genesis 5:24

16

Such legends about outstanding personalities were replete before and at the time of Jesus. Josephus writing in ***Antiquities*** says of Moses: "a cloud suddenly stood over him and he disappeared in a certain valley, although he wrote in the holy books that the died, which was done out of fear, lest they should venture to say that, because of his extraordinary virtue, he went to God." Josephus also mentions that some people thought that Moses "had been taken to the divinity."

According to J. Jeremias in **moyses**: *"These went up to heaven: Enoch, Moses and Elijah."*

THE VIRGIN BIRTH

The virgin birth of Jesus is regarded, perhaps, as the most powerful of all miracles supporting the claim for his divinity. Maurice Wiles, Regius Professor of Divinity and Canon of Christ Church, Oxford, and Chairman of the Church of England Doctrine Commission, writes in his article ***Christianity without Incarnation?*** in the book, ***The Myth of God Incarnate:***

"When around the beginning of this century, doubts were expressed about the literal truth of virginal conception of Jesus, these were frequently treated as direct attacks upon the doctrine of incarnation. The virgin birth was so firmly regarded as the means by which the incarnation was effected that the two were widely regarded as standing of falling together."

Strong and irrefutable arguments have down the pages of history been presented against the doctrine of incarnation, i.e. the belief that God Almighty took the human form as Jesus of Nazareth. The arguments range from the Qur'ânic which draw the parallel of the creation of Adam from no-father and no mother, and the conception of Elizabeth, the wife of Zachariah, who barren and having passed menopause, did yet give birth to John. In the case to Zachariah, the Qur'ân says:

"Thus doth Allâh accomplish what he willeth."

Qur'ân 3:40

And in the case of Mary the Qur'ân says:

"Even so: Allâh createth what He willeth: When He hath decreed a plan, He but saith to it "Be" and it is!"   Qur'ân 3:47

But these are scriptual arguments; they are for a people who have faith. There are those who have dismissed the whole thing as purely mythological, and have presented many similar claims of virgin birth for pagan divinities prior to Jesus Christ. Persus of Greece was supposed to have been born by a Danae. The virgin Rhea Silvia gave birth to Romulus of Rome. The Egyptian Horus was born by Isis, the immaculate virgin queen of heaven. The argument is that these legends were current in the Mediterranean region about the time of Jesus was most likely equally legendary.

Rationalist interpreters of the Bible have found fault with the current translations, and have sought to place on record what they believe is the more correct rendering of the original text. Marcello Craveri accuses the Church Fathers of launching into a search for every passage in the Scriptures which could be seen in any way to foretell the coming of a "Son of God" through virgin birth. As an example Craveri refers to Isaiah 7:14 as the most quoted prophecy regarding the virgin birth:

"Therefore the Lord himself will give you a sign. Behold a virgin shall conceive, and bear a son, and shall call his name Immanuel."

Craveri argues that the prophecy had nothing to do with the birth of Jesus. The original text speaks, ***not of a "virgin" but of a "young woman"***. The Revised Standard Version of the Bible agrees with Marcello Craveri in this respect. The actual meaning of the prophecy is admitted to be difficult by the same Christian commentators who claim that it refers to Jesus. Craveri says that is as expected "since the excerpt had nothing to do with the birth of Jesus. It is the ending of a discussion that Isaiah says he had with King Ahaz, in which the prophet reassured the king of the imminent destruction of his two enemies, the Kings of Syria and Israel".

Another rationalist G.Vermes in ***Jesus the Jew*** argues that "virgin" even as applied to Mary could well have originally meant one too young for child-bearing, just as Sarah, Hannah and Elizabeth were old, or barren.

Lastly we have the opinion of a scientist and a medical practitioner regarding the general question of conception by a virgin. Dr. T.H. Van de Velde M.D. writing in his best selling book on sexology, ***Ideal Marriage***, says: "There are numerous though; of course, exceptional instances on record of impregnation or conception following the penetration of sperm cells into the female genitalia without complete ***immissio penis*** or entrance of the male organ. Such cases are of great practical importance. They plainly prove two things; ***Firstly***, that under certain circumstances impregnation can result even when the hymen remains unbroken. And ***secondly***, that a ***spermatozoon*** can reach the female organs indirectly, e.g. through the contact of a finger..."

The profundity of all these speculations, medical, scientific or rational, is undoubted; but it is the Qur'ân which spells out the truth in words simple enough for babes to understand:

"The similitude of Jesus before Allâh is as that of Adam: He created him from dust, then said to him: "Be": and he was. The truth (comes) from Allâh alone; so be not of those who doubt."   Qur'ân 3:59-60

JESUS - Prophet from Nazareth the servant of God

"Christ disdaineth not to serve and worship God"
         Qur'ân 4:172

The Bible bears out this Qur'ânic truth. In number of places we note Jesus saying with pride that he has been sent by God, and a number of times he is referred to as the "servant of God"

"And this is eternal life, that they may know thee the only true God, and Jesus Christ whom thou has sent."

John 17:3

Thus Jesus in befitting humility addresses God as "the only true God", and he himself has been sent as a messenger of God.

"God having raised up his servant sent him to you first, to bless you in turning every one of you from your wickedness."

Acts 3:26

"The God of Abraham and of Isaac and of Jacob, the God of our fathers, glorified his servant Jesus, whom you delivered up and denied in the presence of Pilate, when he had decided to release him."

Acts 3:13

"And now, Lord, look upon their threats, and grant to thy servants to speak thy word with all boldness, while thou stretches out thy hand to heal, and sign and wonders are performed through the name of thy holy servant Jesus."

Acts 4:30

The sick are healed, signs and wonders are performed: who does all this? *It is the hand of God*. The name of Jesus may be invoked, but that is only instrumental, as an interceder, for he at best is only "the holy servant of God."

Jesus is reported to say according to the Gospels: *"Whoever receives me, receives not me but Him who sent me."*

Mark 9:37

The Qur'ân expressed the same sense in the following words: *"He who obeys the Apostle (Muhammad - (SAW)) obeys Allâh."*

Qur'ân 4:80

And in the following verse the Prophet Muhammad is told by Allâh:

"Say: If ye do love God, follow me: God will love you and forgive you your sins: for God is oft-forgiving, Most Merciful."

Qur'ân 3:31

20

In the Gospel of John Jesus says: *"My food is to do the will of him who sent me, and to accomplish His work."*

John 4:34

That is indeed the literal translation of the word **ISLAM**, which means, *"Submission to the will of God."*

"My teaching is not mine, but his who sent me; if any man's will its to do His will, he shall know whether the teaching is from God or whether I am speaking on my own authority. He who speaks on his own authority seeks his own glory; but he who seeks the glory of Him who sent him is true, and in him there is no falsehood." John 7:14-18

"He who receives you receives me, and he who receives me receives Him who sent me. He who receives a prophet because he is a prophet receives a prophet's reward, and he who receives a righteous man because he is a righteous man shall receive a righteous man's reward." Matthew 10:40-41

We thus see on the strength of Christ's own testimony that he is a righteous servant of God, a prophet sent by God, an apostle. Time and time again he repeats that he has not come on his own authority, that he does not even act or speak on his own authority; but that he says and acts in fulfillment of the commandment and the will of God who has sent him. These are the true qualities of a prophet and messenger of God. And that indeed is what his followers who saw him and lived with him took him to be.

Read the Gospels:

"When the people saw the sign which he had done, they said, "This is indeed the prophet who is to come into the world."

John 6:14

"But when they tried to arrest him, they feared the multitude, because they held him to be a prophet." Matthew 21:46

"And the crowds said, "This is the prophet Jesus from

21

Nazareth of Galilee." Matthew 21:11

"And he said to them, "What things?" And they said to him, "Concerning Jesus of Nazareth, who as a prophet mighty in deed and word before God and all the people."

Jesus not only denied that he was God, but also refused to be considered even good:

"And as he was setting out on his journey, a man ran up and knelt before him, and asked him, "Good Teacher, what must I do to inherit eternal life?" And Jesus said to him, "Why do you call me good? No one is good but God alone." Mark 10:17-18

A PROPHET TO ISRAEL

We have seen from the extracts we have reproduced from the Bible the Jesus was sent by God.

To whom was he sent? To the World? - **Let the Bible speak:**

"And Jesus went away from there and withdrew to the district of Tyre and Sidon. And behold. A Cannanite woman from the region came out and cried, "Have mercy on me, O lord, Son of David; my daughter is severely possessed by demon." But he did not answer her a word. And his disciples came and begged him saying, "Send her away, for she is crying after us." He (Jesus) answered, "I was sent only to the lost sheep of Israel." Matthew 15:21-24

When Jesus was despatching his twelve chosen disciples to go out and spread the Gospel he instructed them to avoid going into non-Israelite towns.

Matthew reports: *"These twelve Jesus sent out, charging them, "Go nowhere among the Gentiles (i.e. non-Jews), and enter no town of the Samaritans, but go rather to the lost sheep of the house of Israel."*   *Matthew 10:5-6*

"Jesus said to them, "Truly, I say to you, in the new world, when the Son of man shall sit on his glorious throne, you who have followed me will also sit on twelve thrones, judging the twelve tribes of Israel."   *Matthew 19:28*

The claim that Jesus Christ is a redeemer of the world from sin is rebutted by his own categorical statement recorded in the Gospel according to John. In prayer to God he declares his own limitations consistent with the general spirit of his mission.

"I am praying for them; I am not praying for the world but for those whom thou hast given me, for they are thine."

John 17:9

If we allow ourselves to judge from the statement of Jesus as reported by Matthew and Mark that he was sent only to the lost sheep of Israel, and his clear instructions to his disciples that they should go nowhere among non-Jews but rather to the lost sheep of the house of Israel, and his prophecy that he and his twelve disciples would be judging the twelve tribes of Israel in the hereafter, we would not be wrong to conclude that the people referred to in Jesus's prayer quoted above must be the same, the Israelites. It is a historical fact that Christianity was not preached to non-Jews until after the conversion of Paul. It was he who insisted on doing that in the face of strong opposition from the chosen apostles of Jesus. They regarded such action as violation of the explicit instructions and practice of the Master. Dr. Marcello Craveri writes in his book *The Life of Jesus*:

"Meanwhile, Paul had come into the picture. With his over-whelming personality and his ambition, he lost no time in interjecting himself among the "pillars" of the community, as he himself rather ironically spoke of James and Peter. Quarrels and conflicts between them and Paul soon arose, especially over the new converts outrageous proposal to carry the religion beyond the borders of Judaism."

Biblical scholar, Dr. Hugh Schonfield, in his book, ***Those Incredible Christians***, writes thus of Paul's conflicts with the genuine original followers of Christ:

" The Saul of today, who used the Roman name of Paul, was seen as the demon-driven enemy of the new David. When eventually he became a prisoner of the Romans, the Christians neither of Jerusalem nor Rome lifted a finger to aid him. None of Paul's efforts including raising funds for the poor saints of Judea, had mitigated opposition to him. For the more intransigent of the legitimate Church Paul was a dangerous and disruptive influence, bent on enlisting a large following from among the Gentiles in order to provide himself with a numerical superiority with the support of which he could set at defiance the Elders at Jerusalem. Paul had been the enemy from the beginning, and because he had failed in his former open hostility he had craftily insinuated himself into the fold to destroy it from within. This he was doing by setting aside the sacred Torah and recruiting anyone willing to join him on the merest profession of belief. He should never have been received; but there were those who were so innocent and unsuspicious that they had not realized what he was up to. And see to what a state of affairs their misplaced confidence had led! The whole Nazorean cause, the cause of Messiah himself, was in jeopardy of being utterly discredited in Israel. Because Paul seemed to be on of its chief spokesmen and was announcing that the Torah was invalid as a means of salvation it would be believed by pious Jews that the followers of Jesus were the worst kind of renegades."

The wisdom of Jesus in restricting his teaching to Israel lay in his desire to preserve the monotheism of Abraham from being contaminated by pagan influences which prevailed all around him among the non-Jews. As far as he was concerned the rest of humanity was not yet ready to receive the whole truth. His fears became more than fully realized when, with

Paul's conversion and consequential missionary activities, not only was the sacred Law of God branded a cursed, but the pagan cults of Mithra, Orpheus, Osiris, Attis etc were systematically absorbed and became part and parcel of official Christianity.

The Church's alleged authority to propagate Christianity to non-Laws (apart from Paul's assertion) derives from the following passages of the Gospels:

"Go therefore and make disciples of all nations, baptizing them in the name of the Father and of the Son and of the holy Spirit teaching them to observe all that I have commanded you; and lo, I am with you always, to the close of the age."   Matthew 28:19-20

"And that repentance and forgiveness of sins should be preached in his name to all nations, beginning from Jerusalem."   Luke 24:47

"And he said to them, "Go into all the world and preach the Gospel to the whole creation. He who believes and is baptized will be saved; but he who does not believe will be condemned."   Mark 16:16

All the three above-quoted passages refer not to the historical Jesus when he lived, preached and walked with his disciples. They refer to the *"risen"* Christ after the so called resurrection, when he appeared to the chosen few. It is known that among the four Gospels which are in the Bible the earliest to be written was that of Mark. The others were written later being based on Mark, but with embellishments added according to the writers' tastes. It is known also that the whole passage in Mark about Jesus's rising from the dead, which includes the instruction, contradicting all his previous ones, of preaching Christianity to non-Jews, is a later addition.

The Encyclopedia Britannica 11th edition vol. 17 page 730 says that the passage was added later, possibly early in the second century to take the place of missing words or words which were regarded deficient.

William Neil writing in Harper's Bible Commentary says:

"If there is any point in gospel criticism about which all the experts are agreed, it is that at this point Mark's gospel ends. The rest of the chapter (19:9-20) is so-called longer Ending to the gospel which does not appear in the oldest manuscripts, and which is a second century pastiche of added excerpts from Matthew, Luke and Acts... *the earliest written evidence of the resurrection is not in the gospels but in St. Paul's first letter to the Corinthians 15:3-8*".

If the passage in the 16th chapter of Mark (verse 9 to 20) is an interpolation, as it is hereby proven and admitted to be, then the whole story of Christ's rising from the dead and ordering his disciples to go and preach to all creation baptizing in the name of the Father, the Son and the Holy Spirit, is a later day addition. The author of the legend as far as can be traced from the reading of the Bible, is St. Paul, for the earliest record is not in the Gospels but in Paul's letter to the Corinthians. As Craveri puts it in *The Life of Jesus:*

"Paul convinced himself that though Jesus had really died, he must have risen, leaving his earthly body behind in order to take on a "spiritual" one... blending his own semi-pagan conception of the assumption of Jesus into a new life as a reward for his virtues with the Jewish doctrine of the necessity of a reconciliation with Yahweh, and a "second covenant", Paul taught that exactly this had been the task of Jesus, and these had been his merits in the eyes of God: a vicarious sacrifice through himself in his saintliness and innocence that expiated the collective guilts of all."

If therefore the basis of the whole story of Jesus's rising from the dead is at its best open to question, if not palpably false, then there is no ground for the belief that Jesus at any historical moment ordered that his gospel should be taught to the gentiles. Equally the reference to the Three Persons of the Trinity attributed to Jesus is baseless.

SALVATION BY BLOOD

The theory is that Adam and Eve sinned by eating the forbidden fruit. Their transgression is inherited by all children of Adam and Eve. Since thus they deprive God of a part of what is due to Him, there is no way to escape the just punishment of God except by restoring the loss that men have imposed on God. The argument would have it that since all the good that can be done is owed to God, nothing is gained by undoing a wrong once committed. Hence only a perfect being, who agrees to be punished for the sins of other men, can mollify God's wrath. Since only God is perfect it must be He then who must take the human form, come forward and allow himself to be tortured and be killed for the faults of his creatrues.

Craveri notes: "Thus we enter the truly staggering vicious circle of a god who punishes himself in order to be able to forgive the men and whom who have offended him!"

"And Jesus called them to him and said to them, "You know that those who are supposed to rule over the Gentiles lord it over them, and their great men exercise authority over them. But it shall not be so among you; but whoever would be great among you must be your servant, and whoever would be first among you must be slave of all. For the Son of man also came not to be served but to serve, and to give his life as a ransom for many." Mark 10:42-45

The above passage is one of the Biblical quotations put forward as an argument for the doctrine of salvation by the blood of Jesus. Let us examine the passage:

1. Jesus declares that he "came not to be served but to serve". In the previous pages we have seen how by word and deed Jesus was proud to serve and worship God. In this passage he would not have anyone believe that he came to be served,

far less to be worshipped.

2. The phrase "to give his life as a ransom for many is obviously a figure of speech in the same vein as "Whoever would be first among you must be slave of all." Surely no one would suggest that Jesus means by "slave" literally that one becomes property to be bought and sold. Similarly it is absurd to interpret "giving one's life as a ransom" as the act of physical death being a sacrifice for the atonement for the sins of others. We often hear of leaders in all walks of life being referred to as sacrificing themselves for their people. It never occur to us to understand by that phrase that their death in any way confers benefit to their people. On the contrary what it all amounts to is that such leaders have spent their lives working for the good of their followers.

This reminds me of a cartoon that appeared in the Egyptian daily, Al-Akhbar, of 19th October 1976. The cartoon depicts a mock funeral procession for a parliamentary candidate. A sprawling banner over the bier reads:

"THE MAN WHO EVERYDAY DIES FOR YOU" A ribbon round a wreath carried in front of the solemn procession reads "TO YOUR LAST RESTING PLACE - A SEAT IN THE NATIONAL ASSEMBLY" someone intones "VOTE FOR HIM!" Among the "mourners" is one who sheds a tear, but his friend beside him reminds him: ***Control yourself, man, this is only for public relations!"***

If therefore Jesus did die on the cross for the sins of men, and if it was true that he was God, then the whole process was stage-acting, for God could not really suffer the tortures, and his death meant nothing to him, for actually he did not die, being God. The whole procedure takes the form of outrageous cheating. And if the exercise was predestined, and Jesus knew it as we are made to believe, and that it was in fulfillment of prophecies and the mission of Jesus, then those who inflicted punishment on him and killed him, should be hailed as benefactors of mankind and the beloved of God for their fulfilling to the letter God's own desires.

Another quotation which is used as further argument to strengthen the doctrine of salvation by blood is this from Luke:

"Blessed be the Lord God of Israel for he has visited and redeemed his people, and has raised up a horn of salvation for us in the house of his servant David, as he spoke by the mouth of his holy prophets from of old, and from the hand of all who hates us."   *Luke 1:68-71*

This is the prophecy of Zachariah when his son John was born. But it is clear that he says it is God who has redeemed his people, by raising among them "a horn of salvation," which is the Messiah who was being expected by the Jew to deliver them "from their enemies", the Roman rulers. The coming of the savior, says Zachariah, is in fulfillment of ancient prophecies. It is distorting the meaning of words to interpet this excepted deliverance from the enemies of the Jews, who were the Roman rulers, as meaning salvation by blood of Jesus. Another alleged testimony for the doctrine of atonement by blood:

"The next day, He (John the Baptist) saw Jesus coming toward him and said, "Behold, the Lamp of God, who takes away the sin of the world!"   *John 1:29*

Granted that these words were not the invention of the inventive John the evangelist (for they are not borne out by any other Gospel) is this not much the same thing as when we speak of any earthly leader: "Here is he who bears all our burdens for us"? or when we advise someone: "You will kill yourself, man, trying to heap on your shoulders the problems of the world!" The taking away of sin is not necessarily the same thing as the forgiveness of sin by the death of Jesus; rather is it by living up to his teachings and treading on his footstep (again a figure of speech) that men shall attain salvation. It is through doing the will of God who sent his servant, Jesus, as a prophet and messenger, as he himself so often said, that men shall be saved. It is through righteousness the doing of what is morally right, according to God's laws, that everyone will save himself. Credit is, however reflected on him who points the way, and indeed he thus becomes the savior of the people.

The teaching of Jesus are what is essential, his suffering in the course of his work is incidental. Are we justified in laying stress on the incidental and ignoring, or even belittling, the essential?

The following passage from the Gospel according to John is believed to put the doctrine of vicarious atonement more forcefully and clearly than any other:

"For God so loved the world that he gave his only Son that whoever believes in him should not perish but have eternal life. For God sent the Son into the world, not to condemn the world, but that the world might be saved through him."

John 3:16

Here we have to appreciate that John's Gospel is very different from the three. It was written much later. It was not intended to be a factual narrative, but rather subjective religious propaganda highly charged with sentimentalism. It was obviously intended to push definite doctrines fanatically adhered to by the writer. By the time this Gospel was being written Pauline Christianity must have been quite prevalent and the writer more than a faithful adherent. In this Gospel the absolute divinity of Christ is stressed, and Jesus is referred to as "The only Son of God." The doctrine of salvation is however even in this Gospel not definitely asserted. At best, one might say, It is glanced at. It is only one whose mind is already made up who will interpet the sentence "For God sent the Son into the world not to condemn the world, but that the world might be saved through him." to mean that it is by his death on the cross: or "whoever believes in him" to mean "believes in his death as expiation for other people's sins."

30

Dr. Hugh Schonfield in ***Those Incredible Christians*** presents to us in graphic terms the value of the Gospel according to John as an authentic record of the life and teaching of Jesus Christ. He says:

"Thus in the Fourth Gospel, as in the letters to the Seven Churches, it is not the real Jesus speaking, but John the Elder who is speaking in his name. The fraud can be detected, however, not only because the Christ of the Fourth Gospel expresses himself in a manner which so often is un-Jewish, but far more because the evidence of the first epistle of John reveals that Jesus speaks in the way the creator of his supposed utterances writes. We have to be very thankful for the existence of that epistle. There is no call for us to be horrified at the idea that a gifted and even spiritually minded Christian, whose work has a place in a collection of what many hold to be inspired documents, could be guilty of such gross deception. It should be clear to us by now that there are several bogus books in the New Testament, and others which are purposefully misleading. Our own moral judgment must not be applied to the literary productions of antiquity, where it was not considered at all improper to forge, interpolate and slant documents in a good cause. John would certainly have believed that his design was righteous and God-guided. He would not doubt for a moment that he had been specially raised up by God for the task to be performed, that he was being led by the Spirit. The remarkable way in which everything was working with him at every stage confirmed it."

PAUL OR JESUS? FAITH OR WORKS?

Consider the Sermon on the Mount. Quite early in the Sermon Jesus made clear his mission:

"Think not that I have come to abolish the law and the prophets; I have come not to abolish them but to fulfil them. For truly, I say to you, till heaven and earth pass away, not an iota, not a dot, will pass from the law until all is accomplished. Whoever then relaxes one of the last

of these commandments and teaches men so, shall be called least in the kingdom of heaven; but he who does them and teaches them shall be called great in the kingdom of heaven. For I tell you unless your righteousness exceeds that of the scribes and the Pharisees, you will never enter the kingdom of heaven." *Matthew 5:17-20*

The sermon on the Mount consists of the most important teachings of Jesus Christ. We can say that there lies true Christianity; that is if we believe that it is Jesus who is the founder of Christianity and not St. Paul.

In the above quoted passage Jesus says that it is impossible to enter the kingdom of heaven "unless your righteousness exceeds that of the scribes and the Pharisees." Now what is the righteousness of the scribes and Pharisees? It is to follow the law to the letter, and what the prophets taught. That is why Jesus said: "Think not that I have come to abolish them but to fulfil them." His task was not to replace the law by something else, but rather to combat the purely legalistic externalization of religion among the Jews by the addition of the spirit of religion. He laid emphasis on TEACHING and DOING when he said: "Whoever then relaxes one of the last of these commandments and _**teaches**_ men so, shall be called the least in the kingdom of heaven; by he who _**does**_ them and _**teaches**_ them shall be called great in the kingdom of heaven."

Those are the teachings of Christ himself; but what does Paul say?

"Eat whatever is sold in the meat market without raising any question on the ground of conscience."
1 Corinthians 10:25

"You are severed from Christ, you who would be justified by law; you have fallen away from grace. For through the Spirit, by faith, we wait for the hope of righteousness."
Galatians 5:4-5

"We ourselves, who are Jews by birth and not Gentile

sinners, yet who know that a man is not justified by works of the law but through faith in Jesus Christ, even we have believed in Christ Jesus, in order to be justified by faith in Christ, and not by works of the law, because by works of the law shall no one be justified."   Galatians 2:15-16

"Likewise, my brethren, you have died to the law through the body of Christ, so that you may belong to another, to him who has been raised from the dead in order that we may bear fruit for God. While we were living in the flesh, our sinful passions, aroused by the law, were at work in our members to bear fruit for death. But now we are discharged from the law, dead to that which held us captive, so that we serve not under the old written code but in the new life of the Spirit."   Romans 7:4-6

"For we hold that a man is justified by faith apart from works of law."   Romans 3:28

The teachings of Paul created controversy early in the history of the Church between his party and that of Jewish Christians who objected to the teaching of the new religion to the uncircumcised Gentiles (i.e. non-Jews) whom they regarded as unclean. Some of the disciples would not even sit at table with the "uncircumcised" who did not keep the law of Israel. Ultimately a meeting was held between the two factions, and a compromise was arrived at whereby it was agreed that no heavy burdens should be placed on the Gentiles who were converted to Christianity from paganism:

"Then it seemed good to the apostles and the elders, with the whole church to choose men from among them and send them to Antioch with Paul and Barnabas."

Acts 15:22

"For it has seemed good to the Holy Spirit and to us to lay upon you no greater burden than these necessary things: that you abstain from what has been sacrificed to idols, and from blood, and from things strangled and

33

from unchastity. If you keep yourselves from these, you will do well. Farewell."

Acts 15:28-29

How comes it then that Paul writes to the Corinthians:

"Eat whatever is sold in the meat market without raising any question on the ground of conscience"? Paul claims to have been appointed an apostle of Jesus in a revelation and that he continues to receive instructions directly from the Master even though those instructions might be contrary to what the disciples received from Jesus in person. Let us examine from Holy Scripture the basis of Paul's claims. This stems from the incident of his conversion to Christianity on his way to Damascus. it should be remembered that St. Paul who was previously called Saul, had been an implacable enemy of Christians before this incident. Which is referred to three times in the Acts of the Apostles, and each time it is differently related.

The first version of the story runs like this:

"Now as he journeyed he approached Damascus, and suddenly a light from heaven <u>flashed about him.</u> And <u>he fell to the ground and heard a voice saying to him,</u> "Saul, Saul, why do you persecute me?" And he said, "Who are you Lord? And he said, <u>*"I am Jesus, whom you are persecuting, but rise and enter the city, and you will be told what you are to do .*</u>" Then men who were tavelling with him stood speechless *<u>hearing the voice but seeing no one."</u>*

Acts 9:3-7

In this version the incident is related by the author of the Acts. The points worth noting are:

a) The light which Paul saw "flashed about him". It is not related that others saw the light, but they did hear the voice.

b) It was Paul who fell to the ground.

c) He and the men who were with him heard the voice, but they saw no one.

34

d) The voice of Jesus ordered him to enter the city and there he "would be told what he was to do."

The second version of the story runs like this as reported in the same book, **The Acts of the Apostles**. But the word are purported to be spoken by Paul before the tribune and the crowd of Jews as he was answering charges of preaching against the law and defiling the temple by bringing Greeks into it.

"As I made my journey and drew near to Damascus, about noon a great light from heaven suddenly shone about me. And I fell to the ground and heard a voice saying to me, "Saul, Saul, why do you persecute me?" And I answered "Who are you, Lord?" and he said to me, "I am Jesus of Nazareth whom you are persecuting." <u>**Now those who were with me saw the light but did not hear the voice of the one who was speaking to.**</u> *And I said, "What shall I do, Lord?" And the Lord said to me, "Rise, and go into Damascus, and there you will be told all that is appointed for you to do."*   Acts 22:6-10

This version agrees with the first version in respect of:

a) The one who fell to the ground was Paul and not those who were with him.

b) What Paul was told was to enter the city and there he would be told what to do.

It however disagrees with the first version in that the first says that those who were with him **heard the voice,** but it does not say that they saw the light. In this second version it is stated that those who were with Paul "**saw the light but did not hear the voice.**"

The third version of this vital incident in Christian history is also contained in Paul's own words as related in the same holy book **The Acts of the Apostles:**

"Thus I journey to Damascus with the authority and commission of the chief priest. At midday, O King, I saw on

the way __*a light from heaven, brighter than the sun, shining*__ *around me and those who journey with me. And* __*when we had*__ __*all fallen to the ground,*__ *I heard a voice saying to me in Hebrew language, "Saul, Saul, why do you persecute me? It hurts to kick against the goads." And I said, "Who are You, Lord?" and the Lord said, "I am Jesus whom you are persecuting. But rise and stand upon your feet; for I have appeared to you for this, to appoint you to serve and bear witness to the things in which you have seen me and to those in which I will appear to you, delivering you from the people and from the Gentiles to whom I send you to open their eyes, that they may turn from darkness to light and from the power of Satan to God, that they may receive forgiveness of sins and a place among those who are sanctified by faith in me."*   Acts 26:12-18

Now here we see great divergences with the statements in chapter 9 and chapter 22 of this very same book.

a) According to this third version it is not Paul alone who saw the light- as related in the first version, but all, as related in the second version.

b) Here Paul says that they all fell to the ground. This contradicts the first and the second versions which relate that it was Paul only who fell.

c) Instead of being instructed by the mysterious voice of Jesus to enter the city where Paul would be told what to do, this version gives detailed instructions as imparted to Paul there and then of being appointed as the Apostle of Jesus who also promises him that he will appear to him again; and violating all of Jesus's teachings to his disciples when he was alive, sends Paul as a special messenger to preach the gospel to non-Jews; and, also contrary to Jesus's teaching during his life-time, teaches justification by faith alone.

Why should Paul be so expansive in this third version? It is because he is here addressing King Agrippa. But we may pause to wonder what we would think of witness who relates one story of the police, changing it a little when he faces the magistrate, and gives a completely different version when the case reaches the High Court. But no one can describe Paul better than the description he has given of himself in his letter to the Corinthians. He says and I quote:

"For though I am free from all men, I have made myself a slave to all, that I might win the more. To the Jews I became as a Jew, in order to win Jews; to those under the law I became under the law - though not being myself under the law- that I might win those under the law. Those outside the law I became as one outside the law - not being without law toward God but under the law of Christ - that I might win the weak. I have become all things to all men, that I might by all means save some, I do it all for the sake of the gospel, that I may share in its blessings."

1 Corinthians 9:19-23

To win converts seems to be the be-all and end all- of St. Paul. The doctrine of the end justifying the means seems here to be carried to extreme absurdity.

St. Paul says:

"The word is near you, on your lips and in your heart (that is, the word of faith which we preach) - because, if you confess with your lips that Jesus is Lord and believe in your heart that God raised him from the dead, you will be saved."   *Romans 10:8-9*

But let us read from the epistle of James, the brother of Jesus about which Hugh Schonfield in ***The Possover Plot*** writes: "The true spirit of Jesus is manifested in the epistle of James in the New Testament."

Says James:

"What does it profit, my brethren, if a man says he has faith but has no works? Can his faith save him? If a brother or sister is ill-clad and in lack of daily food, and one of

37

you says to them, "Go in peace, be warmed and filled,"
without giving them the things needed for the body, what
does it profit? So faith by itself, if it has no works, is dead.
But some one will say, "You have faith and I have works."
Show me your faith from your works, and I by my works
will show you my faith. You believe that God is one; you
do well. Even the demons believe-and shudder. Do you want
to be shown, you foolish fellow, that faith apart from work
is barren? Was not Abraham our father justified by works,
when he offered his son Isaac upon the altar? You see that
faith was active along with his works, and the scripture
was fulfilled which says, "Abraham believed God, and it
was reckoned to him as righteousness;" and he was called
the friend of God. You see that a man is justified by works
and not by faith alone. And in the same way was not Rahab
the harlot justified by works when she received the messengers
and sent them out another way? For as the body apart from
the spirit is dead, so faith apart from works is dead."

James 2:14-26

These doctrine which truly depict the teaching of Jesus are in direct conflict with those propounded by St. Paul. No wonder does Paul insist in undisguised wrath:

"And what I do I will continue to do, in order to
undermine the claim of those who would like to claim that
in their boasted mission they work on the same terms as
we do. For such men are false apostles, deceitful workmen,
disguising themselves as apostles of Christ And no wonder,
for even Satan disguises himself as an angel of light. So
it is not strange if his servants also disguise themselves
as servants of righteousness. Their end will correspond
to their deeds." 2 Corinthians 11:12-15

Paul's motive thus made even clear. He wants to win converts by hook or by crook, and to undermine the claim to Christ's discipleship of all those worthy comapnions of Jesus who studied at his feet and shared all the tribulations with him. What are we to do when we are faced with such obvious contradictions between two contending parties both claiming to be representing Christ? The wise thing to do is to go to the Master himself and study those of his sayings which are plain and clear enough to be credible and which generally reflect his overall teaching and life. Jesus's most sustained preaching is embodied in what is called the Sermon on the Mount. His most categorical statement regarding the law and works is contained in Matthew chapter 5. With regard to Jesus's own view on those who claim to be representing him while at the same time distort his teachings. **Jesus is reported to say:**

"Not every one who says to me, "Lord, Lord" shall enter the Kingdom of heaven, but he who does the will of my Father who is in heaven. On that day many will say to me, "Lord, Lord, did we not prophecy in your name, and cast out demons in your name and did many wonderful works in your name?" And then will I declare to them, "I never knew you: depart from me, you evildoers." Every one then who hears these words of mine and does them will be like a wise man who built his house upon the rock; and the rain fell, and the floods came, and the winds blew and beat upon the house, but it did not fall, because it had been founded on the rock. And every one who hears these words of mine and does not do them will be like a foolish man who built his house upon the sand: and the rain fall, and the floods came, and the winds blew and beat against that house, and it fell; and great was the fall of it."

Matthew 7:21-27

These are the concluding words in the Sermon on the Mount. They are forthright and unambiguous. Who are these "evildoers", these foolish men who will not follow the teachings of Jesus which are based on the fulfillment of the law and the prophets and doing the will of God? Who are these men who pretend to perform miracles and to be apostles of Christ, and yet contradict his teachings by preachings justification by faith in the salvation by blood without doing what Jesus ordered them to do, namely to live to the law and the teachings of the prophets? Who are these men who use Jesus's name and yet will be denied by him? He that has understanding let him understand. Let us not be like the foolish man who built his house upon the sand lest we fall, for great will be the fall of it.

GUIDE INTO ALL THE TRUTH

Jesus Christ's teaching is quite substantial, but his short life and the immaturity of his people prevented him from completing the mission on which he had been sent into the world. It is possible also that his mission was by necessity of a limited nature, to pave the way for what was to come. Under either circumstances he had to confess *"I Have many things to say to you, but you cannot bear them now. When the Spirit comes, he will guide you into all the truth."*

The gospel according to John reports the following as part of a speech which Jesus made to his disciples during the Last Supper.

"But now I am going to him who sent me; yet none of you asks me, "Where are you going?" But because I have said these things to you, sorrow has filled your hearts Navertheless I tell you the truth: It is to your advantage that I go away, for if I do not go away, the Counsellor will not come to you: but if I go, I will send him to you. And when he comes, he will convince the world of sin and of righteousness and of judgment: of sin, because they do not believe me; of righteousness, because I go to the Father, and you will see me no more; of judgment, because the ruler of this world is judged. I have many things to say to you, but you cannot bear them now. When the Spirit comes, he will guide you into all the truth; for he will not speak on his authority, but whatever he hears he will speak, and he will declare to you things that are to come. He will glorify me, for he will take what

By this Jesus is informing his disciples that he is about to leave the world, that he has not accomplished his mission, but that another will come after him to teach the whole truth. That other one is called by various names according to the various versions of the Bible. The Revised Standard Version which I have been using throughout this essay calls him Counsellor. King James's Authorized Version calls him Comforter. Whatever the title, the "Counsellor" was described by Jesus as the person who:

a) would come after him

b) would convince the world of sin and of righteousness and of judgment;

c) would guide mankind into all the truth;

d) would not speak on his own authority, but whatever he would hear he would speak;

e) would prophecy;

f) would glorify Jesus Christ.

Let us examine this prophecy of Jesus as reported by John's Gospel without any preconceived notions, and with perfect objectivity. Many Christians with minds fully indoctrinated by Church authorities take it for granted that the prophecy refers to the Holy Ghost, or the Holy Spirit, the third Person of the "ever blessed incomprehensible Trinity". This belief is strengthened by the parenthetical insertion of the title, the Holy Spirit, after Counsellor in John 14:25. with "the accumulated errors of fourteen centuries of manuscripts copying", as the editors of the Revised Standard Version themselves admit, it is easy to imagine the interpolation of such a title as the Holy Spirit either as an explanation believed by the original writer, or by any of the numerous manuscript copyist down the centuries as the likely intention of Christ. The Holy Ghost or Spirit is the one that is believed to have filled the disciples of Jesus and after them the Church authorities, generation after generation until today. What the Church does and says is through the guidance and inspiration of the Holy Spirit as prophesied by Jesus in the above quoted passage.

Since Christianity is divided into countless contradictory Churches or sects, it is difficult to see in which one of them is the Holy Spirit working. Every one of these Churches claims that it alone is the true inheritor of the Church alleged to have been established by Christ when he called Peter "the rock on which he built his Church." Each Church has fundamental differences with other churches. Even within the same church, say the Roman Catholic Church, the best organized and the most monolithic of them all, we find different and contradictory doctrines and commandments issuing at different periods. Men and Women who at one historic period have been ex-communicated, condemned and even burnt at the stake, have by the same infallible Holy Church been not only reinstated, but also canonized as saints, at other historic periods. The history of Christendom is full of such examples. And all this time we are to believe that it is the Holy Spirit, who, according to the Church teachings, is God who never errs, is guiding all these conflicting men who issue conflicting doctrines and rulings through the centuries!

The "Counsellor", Jesus said, would speak on God's authority and not on his own. That statement alone is enough to demolish the theory that the prophecy refers to the Holy Spirit. The Holy Spirit, according to Christian teaching, is God. He could not be said to be speaking on an authority not his own. This could only be said of mortal man, a man inspired, a prophet. That man would bring clear teachings as to sin, righteousness and judgement. His teachings would be universal, not for the "lost sheep" of any particular tribe, but for the world. To be universal and complete those teachings must be clear and precise, and should be on a permanent record which is not subject to interpolation or change, so that all differences that might arise down the centuries could be resolved by reference to that impeccable record.

Finally, Jesus said, the Counsellor would glorify him. Since the departure of Christ from mortal life, it is a historical fact that no one has appeared in any part of the globe who closely fits in with the qualifications enumerated in the above prophecy of Jesus except the Prophet Muhammad. It is he who has claimed, and indeed has achieved, the completion of the mission of Jesus and all the previous prophets. The Encyclopedia Britannica calls him "The Most successful of all prophets." It is he who has convinced the world of sin, of righteousness and of judgement. It is he who has guided us into all the truth - for he is the Spirit of Truth. Indeed even as a youth before he became aware of his future mission he was known by his fellow-citizens of pagan Mecca as Al-Amin, i.e. the Truthful. As an elderly man of over sixty, three months before his death, having completed his God given task he told the assembled multitude, now all Muslims, quoting Allâh's words (for he spoke not on his own authority):

"Today I have completed and perfected for you your religion."   *Qur'ân 5:3*

Having guided the world into all the truth he recited Allâh's own words:

And say: *"Truth has arrived, and Falsehood perished: for Falsehood is bound to perish."*   *Qur'ân 17:81*

THE BIBLE AND THE QUR'ÂN

Jesus confessed that he had not said all that he wanted to say, but that he that was to come would do so and complete the work. The teachings of Muhammad on sin, on righteousness and on judgement are embodied in the Qur'ân, a book that is unique in the world in its purity, lack of contradictions and in its inimicability. Since its revelation to the illiterate Prophet 1400 years ago not one word has changed, and it will not change, by the grace of Allâh, till the day of judgment. Sir William Muir, a well known critic of Islam, writing in his book, *The Life of Muhammad*, says: *"There is probably in the world no other book which has remained twelve centuries with so pure a text."* Since Sir William wrote that another two centuries have rolled by and the truth has remained.

With regard to the Bible, however, there is not and cannot be consistency, for the Bible is not one book but a collection of many books wirtten by numerous writers, many of whom are not even known. There is even disagreement among the Christian Churches as to the books which are accepted as canonical i.e. authorized by church elders as to have been *inspired,* not *revealed* as the Qur'ân was. The writings even in single book may be contradictory, as we have noted the example of the conversion of Paul as recorded in *The Acts of the Apostles.*

Hugh Schonfield wirting in his book, *Those Incredible Christians,* says:

"Within the covers of the Bible we can meet with forgeries, manipulations and deliberate inventions just as much as outside it. Scholarship is well aware of this; but when a biblical work, especially in the New Testament, is evidently not by the person claming to be the author everything is done to avoid using the word forgery. The same is true of sayings attributed to Jesus and know not to be genuine. We speak of such books as by someone of the Pauline or Petrine school of thought, of changed or invented sayings as "secondary". If we did not employ evasions it would appear that the Holy Spirit was an accessory to fraud.

"It is on record, however, that down to the final determination of the canon of Scripture some of the books which are in the Bible were disputed. It was argued by quite orthodox Christians of the early centuries that certain books were not genuine productions of the apostolic authors by whom they purported

44

to have been written. Occasionally the forger's name was suggested. Paul mentions that in his own lifetime false letters in his name were in circulation. What had to be suited was what was deemed to be the interest of the Church. Considerations having nothing to do with truthfulness were at work in the slant given to compositions and in the sentiments contrary to their own attitudes which various persons of note were made to express. All this kind of this was a commonplace for the early Christians as well. This was the way the game of promotion and indoctrination was played. For those without scruples, who believe that ends justify means, it is so still."

The originals of the books of the Bible are absent and unknown, hence the numerous versions. Admittedly the books as at present available are the works of ordinary human writers. However some words which are of divine origin may be discernible. But so mixed are these, and so much interpolation has taken place that it is now almost impossible to tell the divine from the human. You cannot tell with any degree of probability which is the word of God, and which is the word of a mere man who had a particular school to uphold or a particular axe to grind. Not so the Qur'ân. Every word is Allâh's own. It is in direct speech as revealed, not just inspired, to the Prophet Muhammad, and exactly as the Prophet recited it straightaway and faithful scribes put it down immediately and others memorized it. A Christian, Dr. John B. Taylor, Reader in Islamic Studies in the Selly Oak Colleges, Birmingham writes in his book ***Thinking About Islam:***

"We have established that Muslims do not speak of Muhammad's writing the Qur'ân, but of his receiving and reciting it. Just as Muhammad himself was concious of the very special character of the Qur'ânic text, so those Muslims after him took pains to preserve with complete accuracy of all the fragments of the Qur'ân. Only two years after Muhammad's death, with the further loss in the battle of some of those who had already memorized the Qur'ân, the various fragments were collected....

A few years later, in the reign of Uthman, the third caliph 'to rule the Muslims after Muhammad's death, a final check was made on the text of the Qur'ân. We can tell how careful and scrupulous the early Muslims were by the fact that even variations in pronunciation from one part of Muslim world to another were disapproved of in the context of reciting the Qur'ân; and so the official text was established in accordance with the dialect of Mecca, and most other versions were destroyed by command of the caliph. Thus we can feel confident that the Qur'ân which we have today is as far as is humanly possible the text which was established within a few years of the Prophet's death."

Those are the views of a Christian critic of Islam. The Qur'ân is the unsullied word of God. That is what Jesus meant when he said of him who was to come: "He will not speak on his authority, but whatever he hears he will speak."

Jesus was insulted not only by his avowed enemies, the Jews, but also unwittingly by those who considered themselves his followers. The Jews accused him of being a child born out of wedlock, and a charlatan. To prove that he was accursed they endeavored to cause his death by crucifixion, a mode of execution considered by them to be damnatory to the soul of the victim. (see Deuteronomy 21:22-23). They denied that he was their promised Messiah.

The Christians on their part, in their overzeal, and deluded by subtle wolves in sheep's clothing, swallowed the teachings of Mithraism, Greek mythology and other contemporary Mediterranean cults, and placed Jesus on the pedestal of a pagan god. Jesus who was the son of man. **_Ben Adam_**, as he was fond of calling himself, a Prophet and a servant of God, was debased into a pseudo polytheistic god, and became surrounded with legends of propitiation by blood, legends which were current at that time within the cults of Osiris, Attis, Adonis and Mithra.

There was nothing new in salvation by blood. All these

46

doctrines were prevalent in the pagan cults in the eastern Mediterranean region before the coming of Jesus Christ and during his lifetime. *What was new, strange and revolting was to graft these myths on the very man who came to abolish them.*

DEATH ON THE CROSS

It was the Prophet Muhammad who came and glorified Jesus. He countered the accusation of the Jews, and tore down the pagan trappings with which Jesus was enshrouded by misguided adherents. He proved that Jesus was no more illegitimate than Adam. His mother Mary whom the Jews castigated as a prostitute was given a place of great honour in the Qur'ân than in the Christian Bible. To the people who believed in the creation of Adam with neither father nor mother why should it be difficult to believe in the creation of Jesus without a father?

"God is able from these stones to raise up children to Abraham."
Matthew 3:9

To the hostile Jews Muhammad confirmed that Jesus was the Christ foretold in the Jews own scripture. He taught that the Jews were speaking an untruth when they claimed to have inflicted an ignoble death on Jesus by hanging him on the cross.

"But they killed him not, nor crucified him, but so it was made appear to them, and those who differ therein are full of doubts, with no (certain) knowledge, but only conjecture to follow. For a surety they killed him not." Qur'ân 4:157

Modern Biblical research proves this Qur'ânic truth. It is known that there are other Gospels which have different versions of Christ's passion from that narrated in the four canonical Gospels. The other Gospels were not approved officially by the Church when the Bible was compiled towards the end of the second century. Lately new light has been cast on the beliefs of the early Christians by the discovery of an old Manuscript in the archives of Istanbul. The discoverer is Dr. Samul Stern of Oxford University. *These early Christians known as Nasoreans or Nazarenes (which tallies with the Qur'ânic name for Christians: "Nasaara")* were predominant to start with. The Nazarenes who claimed descent from Jesus's first disciples came into conflict with Pauline Christians (who followed Paul) and were driven out of Palestine into Syria around 62 A.D. The Nazarenes regarded Jesus as a great prophet and righteous man. They accused St. Paul of heretically substituting Roman customs for the authentic teachings of Jesus and proclaiming him to be God. They refused to celebrate Christmas which they regarded as a pagan feast.

The version of Christ's Passion contained in the manuscript is that Judas tricked the Jews by substituting another man in place of Jesus. This other man vehemently denied before Herod and Pilate the charge that he claimed to be the Messiah (Christ). According to this version it was Herod and not Pilate, who took a basin of water and washed his hand of the accused man's blood to show that he did not find any guilt in him. Then Herod locked up the supposed Jesus for the night; but the next morning he was seized upon by the Jews who tortured him and ultimately crucified him.

The version of the story of crucifixion makes the pathetic lamentations attributed by the canonical Gospel to Jesus on the cross more sensible. For an ordinary unknown man to behave in such a way is excusable. But for the man of God to declare at the time of trial, or even for a leader of a people with guts in him, to cry out aloud in front of a crowd: "My God, my God why hast thou forsake me?" is to say the least below the dignity of a leader.

If the crucified man was Jesus, and if Jesus was God who knew that He had come down to earth *in order to be crucified for the sins of humanity,* the absurdity would be shattering.

Upton Sinclair writes in his book *A Personal Jesus:*

"You perceive that those who tell the story cannot make up their mind whether Jesus is God or whether he is man. Truly it is difficult problem, once you admit such a thing as the possibility that God may take on the form of a man and come down to earth. When he becomes man, is he man or is He still God? And how can He be betrayed, when He knows He is going to be betrayed? The legend never answers clearly, for basically it is an absurdity and there can be no answer, nor even any rational thought on such a subject.

"If Jesus is God, He knows everything in advance. But in that case the procedure means nothing to Him; He is like an actor going through a role, and it must have been a rather tedious role to Omniscience. Is He doing it for the entertainment of children? If so, why not encourage the children to grow up mentally and face the truth? On the other hand. If he is a man and has the mind of a man, then he no longer knows the truth, he no longer possesses the comfort of the Omniscience. The legend requires that we shall believe both these things at the same time, but manifestly, a man cannot know something and at the same time grope half-blindly as we human beings are doing all through our lives."

The riddle which perplexes honest and intelligent readers of the Gospels like Upton Sinclair is resolved by the Nasorean version of the story of crucifixion. By that version Jesus is absolved from the cowardice, fickleness and shallowness of faith in God so shamfully and cowardly demonstrated by the crucified man. The fickleness and defection of the desciples as reported in the Gospels also fall into position if we take it that the crucified man was not their Messiah. The disciples are therefore cleared from the charges of cowardice, treachery, falsehood and lack of faith in their leader at the most critical time. The man they sold, denied or doubled was truly unknown to them. He was not their Master.

The *"apocryphal"* Gospel of Barnabas reports that it was *Judas who was crucified* in place of Jesus, and *the Basilidon sect* of the early Christian believed that it was *Simon the Cyrene who was crucified,* not Jesus. According to all the three synoptic Gospels it was this man who was made to carry the cross for Jesus. Only John makes Jesus carry his cross. This is a significant point.

Other scholars basing their research on the canonical Gospel have different versions of the crucifixion. One such is Biblical scholar Dr. Hugh Schonfield, who has forwarded his findings in his highly controversial book That Passover Plot. He maintains that it was Jesus who was nailed on the cross, but that he did not die there; he only appeared dead by taking a drug which is described in Matthew's Gospel as vinegar.

"And about the ninth hour Jesus cried with a loud voice, "Eli, Eli, la ma sabach-thani?" that is, "My God, my God, why hast thou forsaken me?" And some of the bystanders hearing it said, "This man is calling Elijah". And one of them at once ran and took a sponge, filled it with vinegar, and put it on a reed, and grave it to him to drink. But the others said, "Wait, let us see whether Elijah will come to save him. And Jesus cried again with a loud voice and yielded up his spirit."   Matthew 27:45-50

That is the description by the evangelist Matthew, or whoever wrote in his name. Schonfield claims that was merely a plot to save Jesus from death by crucifixion. The drug described as vinegar was given to induce a deathlike state. According to the Gospel Jesus remained on the cross for three hours only, while it was normal for a man to take days of lingering agony before his death in that type of execution. Then according to plan, a rich disciple, Joseph of Arimathea, appeared before the Roman Governor Pilate and requested for the body, which was turned over to him. Anthropologist Michael J. Harner of California University corroborating Schonfield says that wine made from the mandrake plant was used in Palestine to induce a deathlike state in persons who were being crucified.

"THEY KILLED HIM NOT"

It is a fact that any careful impartial reader of the four Gospels which are in Bible will derive strong evidence to show that the man who was put on the cross did die on corss, but only appeared to have died. In those same Gospels, there is also overwhelming evidence, in spite of the writers' own belief to the contrary, that it was possible, and indeed likely, that the crucified man was not Jesus Christ at all.

It is a fact that Jesus was not a well-known person at that time in Jerusalem. To the people who were hunting for him, he was a stranger, a rustic from Galilee. He had been preaching his faith for only two or three years, wandering from place to place with no fixed abode. (Matthew 8:20). During that time he could not have visited Jerusalem more than a few times. The earliest Gospel, Mark says he had been there only once, while the latest, John, says four times. So little known was he that it is related Judas had to point out to his would-be captors by pretending to kiss him. Thus it would be nothing unusual if they mistook somebody else for Jesus. The Gospels tell us that when he was arrested all his disciples left him alone and ran away. Even his closest disciple, Peter, denied any knowledge of him, saying: "I do not know this man." (Matthew 26:74). It is difficult to believe that among all his disciples whom he himself had especially selected with due care, there could not have been a single one who even acknowledged that he knew him. To say that this was in fulfillment of a prophecy is to bow to faith, and to stretch reason to breaking point.

Moreover the answers that the accused gave in court during cross examination were not such as to indicate that he was Jesus Christ. At best the accused prevaricated All the three synoptic Gospels describing the court scene failed to produce one piece of evidence which would prove the identity of the accused. Luke says that when he was ordered: "If you are the Christ, tell us," his answer was merely: "If I tell you, you will not believe; and if I ask you, you will not answer."

When he was asked a point blank question : *"Are you the Son of God?" he retorted: "You say that I am."*

Matthew reports: *"And the high priest stood up and said, "Have you no answer to make? What is it that these men testify against you.' But Jesus was silent. And the high priest stood up and said, "I adjure you by the living God, tell us if you are the Christ, the Son of God.' Jesus said to him, "You have said so. But I tell you hereafter you will see the Son of man seated at the right hand of Power, and coming on the clouds of heaven."*

Matthew 26:62-64

Mind you, these narrative even in their original form were written decades after the events, and are related by men who sincerely believe that it was Jesus Christ who was crucified, and yet even they have produced the evidence of only one man, Judas, a shady informer; and that evidence was not given under oath in open court, but merely by implication, a kiss purported to indicate Jesus Christ from among a crowd to a frenzied mob of fanatics.

When we take into serious consideration this reasoning, together with previously related versions narrated by the Gospels other than those include in the Bible and the ancient manuscripts recently discovered which tell of early Christian beliefs that Jesus was not Crucified, the truth of the Qur'ân becomes crystal clear:

"But they killed him not, nor crucified him, but so it was made to appear to them, and those who differ therein are full of doubts, with no (certain) knowledge, but only conjecture to follow. For a surety they killed him not."

Qur'ân 4:157

And the Qur'ân was revealed to an unlettered man fourteen centuries ago. Modern Western scholars now accept the Qur'ânic version of the story of Jesus.

THE LAW AND THE LICENSE

When Jesus foretold the coming of the Counsellor or Comforter who would convince the world of sin because "they did not believe him", he was only speaking the truth. For he had come to the Israelites who were strict in the observance of the letter of the law. Try as he would have failed to convince them of the need to temper their obsession with the mechanics of religion with some spiritual values. He tried to make them appreciate the difference between man-made restrictions and the eternal laws of God.

"You leave the commandment of God, and hold fast the tradition of men."   *Mark 7:8*

Jesus did not bring any new law. His mission was to fulfil the law of Moses. But when he offered his interpretation of the law, the controversy arose. A party of his disciples thought that since he was an Israelite who kept the law and would not alter even "an iota, not a dot" as he himself used to say, it was absolutely necessary for his followers to stick to the law, even as to circumcision, the forbidden foods such as pork and blood, observance of ritual slaughtering and the sanctifying of Saturday as the Sabbath. Another party, St. Paul at their head, argued that since Christ had brought no law they were free from the requirements of the law, for the blood of Jesus on the cross had liberated them from "that slavery", what was necessary was merely to believe that Jesus had died for them. That was salvation enough. To impress the belief in mind and soul of the believer, a procedure was evolved called the Eucharist, the Communion or the Mass. In this solemn ceremony, termed Holy Sacrament, as an outward sign of inward and spiritual grace, sanctified (i.e. made holy) bread and wine are partaken as ***the body and blood of Jesus:***

The Gospel of Matthew relates:

"Now as they were eating, Jesus took bread, and

blessed and broke it, and gave it to the disciples and said, "Take, eat; this is my body, "And he took a cup, and when he had given thanks he gave it to them, saying, "Drink of it, all of you; for this is my blood of the covenant, which is poured out for many for the forgiveness of sins. "
                                                    Matthew 26:26-28

Upton Sinclair in his book *A Personal Jesus* comments on the above quoted verses thus:

"From this has come a procedure called the Eucharist, the Communion, the Mass: a ceremony of unimaginable solemnity. Instead of sacrificing a helpless lamb, it is the body of Jesus which was sanctified on the cross, it is his blood which washed, and by supernatural transformation the bread and wine become his body and blood, and you reverently eat and drink, or let the priest do it for you. Billions of words have been spent in argument, and thousands of tomes have been printed over that question of just how this metamorphosis takes place. There is transubstantiation and there is consubstantiation and there is a third variety called impanation. The Catholics hold for what they call the Real Presence; that is, they say that the bread and wine become the actual physical body and blood, even though their appearance remains the same as bread and wine. All devout Catholics have to go once a week and witness this act performed by the priest, and then they know that their souls are safe from hell fire. I don't want to hurt anyone's feelings, and so I content myself with saying that I don't believe Jesus would have had any interest in the procedure."

Marcello Cravery says on the same subject in his book. *The Life of Jesus;*

"No great effort is required to recognize the affinities between the stages of Orphic initiation (catechists, fasting, purification) and those of the Christian novitiate: preparation for the 'mystery' of the Eucharist, fasting, confession, and absolution of sins. But the replacement of the sacred animal with the very person of Christ makes the ceremony grotesque and horrifying. If Jesus is to be considered a human being, the Lord's Supper assumes the characteristic of a cannibal ritual; if Jesus is to be considered the Son of God, the pure and exalted idea of God held by Jesus degenerates into belief in a ruthless god who demands the savage, perpetually renewed sacrifice of his chosen Son.

"Once Paul's innovation had gained acceptance, even the agape of the Apostles lost both its meanings, the eucharistic (gratitude to the deity) and the commemorative (of Jesus) by becoming part of the 'mystery' of Communion. The bread and the wine were made symbols of the person of Jesus: more specifically of his body and his blood.

"The text of the Gospels was then filled out with the additions made by Paul, who, violating historical truth to meet a theological exigency, and declaring with great shamelessness that everything had been directly reported to him by Jesus himself, caused Jesus to say, after breaking of bread: "Take, eat; this is my body, which is broken for you, and when he makes the libation with the wine: "This cup is the new testament (convenant) in my blood."

The proof that the story of the Eucharist or the Lord's Supper was added to the Gospels (Matthew 26:26-29, Mark 14:22-25 and Luke 22:17-19) by Paul is contained in St. Paul's own letter to the Corinthians:

"For I receive from the Lord what I also delivered to you, that the Lord Jesus on the night when he was betrayed took bread, and when he had given thanks, he broke it, and said, "This is my body which is for you. Do this in remembrance of me." " This cup is the new covenant in my blood. Do this, as often as you drink it, in remembrance of me." For as often as you eat this bread and drink the cup, you proclaim the Lord's death until he comes."

1 Corinthians 11:23-26

We have to remember that St. Paul was not Jesus's disciple

when he was alive. He does not even claim to have ever met him personally. He bases his right to speak on his behalf on the visions which he claims to have experienced, and that experience is related in the *Acts of the Apostles* three times, and each time it is differently narrated.

PROPER PERSPECTIVE

With the coming of the Prophet Muhammad matters were put in their proper perspective. The pure Judaism of Moses was reinstated, and Christianity was cleansed of Paulinism. Both were recast in their original imperishable mould of Islam. Muhammad taught with absolute clarity on sin, righteousness and judgment. He removed the many rabbinical restrictions under which the Jews were groaning. He made it clear that some of these had been imposed on them because of their own obstinacy and transgression, and others had been the creation of their priests who had invented such laws and commandments for the sake of a more effective control over their lives. On the other hand he did not leave the people to grope in darkness not knowing what to do by merely referring them to some ancient scripture whose authenticity as open to doubt because of numerous additions, subtractions and changes. That would have made confusion worse confounded. He came with the Qur'ân whose other name was "Furqân" or the **"Criterion"** which distinguished truth from falsehood. He brought a law, the True Law of God, which gave man freedom from the Jewish restrictions but did not grant the license which Paul had unleashed;

"For that would have been another type of slavery, indeed a worse type, because that was mental and spiritual slavery, license to the body but imprisonment of the intellect and the soul".

Allâh says in the Qur'ân

"With my punishment I visit whom I will; but my mercy

extends to all things. That (mercy) I shall ordain for those who do right, and practice regular charity, and those who believe in our signs; those who follow the Apostle, the unlettered Prophet, whom they find mentioned in their own (scriptures), in the Torah and the Gospel; for he commands them what is just and forbids them what is evil; he allows them as lawful what is good and prohibits them from what is bad; he releases them from their heavy burdens and from the yokes that are upon them. So it is those who believe in him, honour him, help him, and follow the light which is sent down with him, it is they who will prosper."

Qur'ân 7:156-157

The Qur'ân laid the greatest emphasis on faith, faith in God, the Compassionate the Merciful, and trust in God's unbounded grace.

"And were it not for the grace and mercy of God not one of you would ever have been pure."   *Qur'ân 24:21*

Someone asked the Prophet whether he should leave his camel to God's care. The Prophet replied: "Tether her, then trust in him."

PAGAN SOURCES

Faith and works are complementary. One without the other is a lopsided monstrosity. Faith, according to the teachings of the Prophet Muhammad, does not consist in believing that another shall bear your burden for you. No one can save another except as a guide and an inspiration. For every one holds in his own hands the means of salvation, "No bearer of a burden shall bear the burden of another," says the Qur'ân. "Whoever does an atom's weight of good shall see it; and whoever does an atom's weight of evil shall see it." That again is the Qur'ân. No priest, not Jesus, nor Muhammad can bear sins for us. It is a doctrine of laziness and self-deception to believe that someone else's sufferings and death shall atone for our sins.

Jesus did not teach that. These were the teachings of the pagan cults prevalent in the Mediterranean region long before Jesus came. *Attis of Phrygia* (later called Galatia in Asia Minor of present-day Turkey), *Adonis of Syria, Dionysius or Becchus of Greece, Mithra of Persia* and *Osiris and Horus of Egypt* were pagan gods with legends about redemption, atonement and resurrection very similar to those ascribed to Jesus. for example:

a) *ATTIS of Phrygia* - was born of a virgin named Nana, and was regarded as the Only Begotten Son and Savior. He was bled to death on March 24th at the foot of a pine tree, and his votaries believed that his blood had renewed the fertility of the earth, and thus brought a new life to humanity. He rose from the dead, and his death and resurrection were celebrated by his followers.

b) *ADONIS of Syria* - Believed to be the Savior, was born of a virgin mother. He also suffered death for the redemption of Mankind. He rose from the dead in Spring.

c) *DIONYSIUS or BACCHUS of Greece* - Another demi god of the pagans. Was termed The Only Begotten Son of Jupiter. He was born of a virgin mother named Demeter on December 25th! to his followers he was the Redeemer and Savior. He called himself the Alpha and Omega. The story of his passion was celebrated every year, and it similarly consisted in death, descent into hell and resurrection.

d) *OSIRIS - the Egyptian god* - was born on 29th December of a virgin mother. He was betrayed by one Typhen and was slain. He was buried, remained in the hell for two or three days and nights. He then rose from the dead.

e) *MITHRA the Persian sun god* - His birth, also of a virgin mother, took place on the 25th of December, Christmas and Easter were the most important fastivals of the Methraists. They had seven sacraments. The most important of which were baptism, confirmation and Eucharistic supper at which the communicants partook of the divine nature of Mithra under the species of <u>bread and wine</u>

With these historical facts in mind one may well wonder whether St. Paul and other Church leaders of his brand derived their doctrines of salvation by blood, atonement, death and resurrection of Jesus, the Eucharist, Trinity, baptism, Christmas and Easter celebrations from Jesus (on whom be peace) and the Holy Spirit or rather from the pagan cults of Greece, Egypt, Syria and Persia which had preceded Christianity. The similarities are too remarkable to be merely coincidental. The movement of the Sun starting its return journey northwards about the 25th of December, depicting birth, and at the equinox (Easter) heralding spring and a coming back to life of nature that had been killed by the wintry blast, could not but strike awe in the untutored barbarians of the northern hemisphere; and their cunning priest knew well enough to create myths and legends which in due course came to be adopted by the Christian Church.

Leo Tolstoi, a true and honest Christian writing in his *Appeal to the Clergy* says: "If the Trinity, and an immaculate conception, and the salvation of mankind by the blood of Jesus, are possible - then anything is possible and the demands of reason are not obligatory."

PROPHECY OF JESUS FULFILLED

If Jesus did not leave for us enough guidance in matters of sin, righteousness and judgment it is for very good reasons which he himself stipulated. (see John 16:5-14 already quoted.) But then he said of him who was to come. "When he comes he will convince the world of sin, and of righteousness and judgment... he will guide you into all the truth."

Jesus said that he that was to come would teach the world about judgment. He himself could set no example to judgeship being himself throughout his life a fugitive from what currently passed as justice. History tells of on spiritual leader after Christ who held the reins of judicial power other than Muhammad, on whom be peace. Shepherded, citizen, husband, father, warrior, administrator, legislator, statesman, judge, saint and prophet the last of them all, with a message direct from Allâh, God Almighty, Muhammad dispensed justice - but his justice was tempered with mercy as befitted one who judged on the authority of the All-Merciful. His chequered life which consisted of as varied phases as is humanly possible in one's lifetime is an inspiration and guidance to all of us, whatever our pursuit. He thus taught by precept and example. He was no mere utopian theorizing recluse out of touch with realities of life, but a practical man of affairs, and at the same time of such sublime spiritual stature as to warrant God's own tribute when He said:

"And thou (O, Muhammad!) standest on an exalted standard of character."   *Qur'ân 68:4*

Once his wife, Aisha, was asked about the character of the Prophet she replied laconically: "His character is the Qur'ân" what a tribute! This man lived his religion, the injunctions which from his Maker.

No wonder Christ had said of him that he would convince the world of righteousness.

The man that Christ foretold was to be a universal messenger; his mission was <u>to convince the world,</u> not merely to save lost members of his tribe, Says Allâh to him, and of him:

"We have not sent thee but as a universal messenger to men, giving them glad things, and warning them against sin, but most men understand not."   *Qur'ân 34:28*

"We sent thee not but a mercy to all creatures."
                                                    Qur'ân 21:107

Jesus said that he had many things to say, but that his people could not bear them at that time. They would be guided into all the truth by him who was to come the Spirit of Truth, whose privilege it was to declare, for all eternity to hear, after the successful completion of his mission:

"There is no prophet after me"

It was he, Muhammad, who was described by God as "The Seal of all the Prophets and Apostles.", When a document is signed and sealed nothing more can be added to it. The Qur'ân and the Life of the Prophet Muhammad are there available for our guidance and inspiration for all times. No one has claimed this finality of Prophethood except Muhammad, and his claim was justified. What was his due he laid claim to in the clearest and simplest terms. What was not his he forbade to be confused with. Consistently did he disclaim any divinity. "Am I anything more than a mortal?" was often on his lips. The Qur'ân instructs him:

Say: "I am but a man like yourselves, but the revelation has come to me that your God is one God: whoever expects to meet his Lord, let him work righteousness, and in the worship of his Lord, admit no one as partner."

Qur'ân 18:110

His duty, he declare - and so did Jesus - was to do the will of Him who has sent him. And that was Islam, submission to the will of God. Muhammad did not claim that he was the founder of a new faith, rather was he merely continuing to a completion the task that was of Jesus. Moses, Abraham and of all the Prophets who had submitted to the will of Allâh. Indeed the Qur'ân says: "And there is not a people but that it had an Apostle." He however was final and universal, for the time had come for finality and universality, and thus was the prophecy of Jesus at the Last Supper fulfilled. The teachings of Muhammad's predecessors had been corrupted by time and man. Their holy books had been polluted by numerous additions, subtractions and alterations. The historical time arrived for the abolition of all tribal and racial faiths. One faith for all men, for all time was now called for. God in His infinite wisdom sent Muhammad with such a faith:

"Verily those who believe, and the Jews and the

Christians and the Sabeans whoever believes in Allâh and the Last Days and acts aright their reward is with their Lord, neither shall they grieve."   Qur'ân 2:62

The world at the time of Christ was not yet in a position to accept the full implication of the teachings of a universal faith. It would have been too violent a change to demand what later could be commonplace. Jesus had to tread the narrow path of tribalism if he were to get a hearing from his Israelites listeners. Consider what he told the Canaanite woman (Matthew 15:21-28), and the instructions he gave to his twelve disciples, (Matthew 10:5-8) as well as his promise to them (Matthew 19:28). Any other course would have likely courted total failure. The circumstances were not auspicious. If you read the Old Testament you will see the difficulty of persuading such a racist community as the Israelites to accept God as the God of all the people.

The Israelites regarded themselves as the chosen children of God, who had been granted the privilege to take other people's lands and properties, by trickery when they were weak and by force when they were strong (Genesis 17:8, Exodus 3:22 and Joshua 6:21,24)

Legends were created under the guise of the Holy Scripture which granted to the Hebrews the status of Herrenvolk, Hitler, most likely, the Dutch Reformed Church of South Africa, most certainly, have received their inspiration from the Old Testament. They believed that God was the Lord of Israel, and are they the beloved chosen children of God destined to lord it over the rest of mankind, particularly the Arabs and the Africans, the Ismaelites and the Hamites.

John Okello the hireling who brought death and terror to Zanzibar in 1964 says in his book that he was inspired by the Bible when he ordered *"The Massacre of Everything that breathed."*

Zionism is the spiritual ancestor of Apartheid and all other forms of Fascism. There is the legend of Noah cursing his son Ham, the ancestor of the Africans (and the Arabs through the Canaanites, the Philistines, the Phoenicians and the Egyptians) and his descendants, to a status of slavery under the Jews and Europeans for eternity. (Genesis 9:18-27) By further scriptural manipulation the Jewish branch of the descendants of Shem had its status enhanced by having God establish his covenant with Isaac, as opposed to Ismael who begot the Arabs. Could such a bigoted people to whom pride of race was everything, to whom the vilest of crimes were virtues sanctified by God so long as they resulted in the perpetuation and domination of their own race over others, could such a people - I humbly ask - be the carriers of a universal message? Most emphatically no! That task could only be tackled by a people with international ties, a people capable of intermingling with others of diverse racial origins. Such a people were the Arabs from whom sprang Muhammad, of Hamitic / Semitic origin, traditionally claiming descent from Ismael, himself born of an African woman from Egypt, Muhammad as an Arab had in him the strains of various Hematic and Semitic peoples who had been inhabiting Arabia even before Abraham came from Chaldea. It is from such Hematic / Semitic ancestors that migratory waves crossed into Africa at various historical periods and gave birth to most of the inhabitants of the continent of Africa of today and the Black people of America. It was this man Muhammad who put an end to the notion of ties of blood as being the most important thing that mattered and bound man together. He abolished tribal and racial discrimination, and instituted a new brotherhood, the brotherhood of faith, and the brotherhood of man. "The aristocracy of old, I trample under my foot, "he said, although he himself came from the noblest family of Arabia. "He who advocates racialism is nothing among us," he announced. When he liberated Mecca from the pagans he declared: "All men are equal like the teeth of a comb. The Arab is no better than a non-Arab. The white has no superiority over the black. All are children of Adam, and Adam is from dust."

Such are some of his saying on the subject of race, a subject which until today plaques many parts of the world.

In Islam no duty is more estimable than the regular congregational prayers; and in them two most important functions are those of the Imam who leads the prayers, and the muezzin who calls the faithful to worship. It was the normal practice of the Prophet to lead the prayers himself, while he assigned the task of Muezzin to Bilal, an Ethiopian ex-slave. The Prophet found nothing incongruous in marrying his cousin to Zaid, his former slave. Nor did he hesitate in appointing Usama a youth of eighteen born of a black African mother as commander of a Muslim army to meet the threat of invasion from the Romans when he was convinced of his suitability for the post. Of Salman the Persian, the Prophet said: "Salman is a member of my family." It may be of interest to note that both Zaid and Salman were convert from Christianity. The first two martyrs of Islam who chose death under torture rather give up their new faith were Yassir, a Yamanite Arab, and his wife, Sumayya, an African.

A universal God, a universal religion, a universal brotherhood could only be taught by such a man and accepted by such a people at such a time. No wonder Islam spread like flare fire.

Thomas Carlyle said in his classical lecture on **Hero as a Prophet:**

"The hsitory of a nation becomes fruitful, soul-elevating and great so soon as it believes. Those Arabs, the man Muhammad, and that one century - is it not as if one spark had fallen, one spark on what seemed dark unnoticeable sand? But lo! the sand proves explosive powder, blazes heaven-high, from Delhi to Granada!"

It was not mere belief that did the trick; it was the type of belief, belief in works, belief in the brotherhood of man and the universality of God's religion. From the Atlantic to the Pacific, from the Caucusus to the Comores, from Senegal to Sinkiang, from Istanbul to Indonesia, all became one brotherhood, all had one all-embracing ideology, all faced towards Mecca, all mixed their bloods and cultures so that differences in race, colour and tongue became completely meaningless. The youngest of all the great religions became the only truly universal one. The only racial groups resisting the attraction of Islam have been those which at all cost would insist on maintaining their racial purity and alleged superiority, and thus have been the greatest contributors to the racial animosities which bedevil the world of today. They are fighting a rearguard action.

COUNSELLOR - COMFORTER - ADMIRABLE

Let us now examine the word Consellor or Comforter, which is the alleged title given by Jesus to the person who was to come after him and guide men into all the truth. As we have already seen, this word has been variously rendered in the different versions of the Bible. The originals of the books of the Bible are non-existent. They are also known to have been written many years after the events they narrate. For example the Gospel according to St. John from which we extract the passage which deals with the prophecy of Christ quoted above is said to have been written roundabout 100 A.D. But the oldest manuscript available was written at least two centuries after the original. The Greek text upon which the Authorized Version was based has been described in the preface to the Revised Standard version as having been "marred by mistakes, containing the accumulated errors of fourteen centuries of manuscript copying." Biblical scholars such as Rudolf Bultman (Protestant) and Father John Lawrence McKenzie (Roman Catholic) agree that parts of the Gospels are not historically true, and that certain sayings of Jesus were created by the early church. Hence it can be seen how easily one word could have various renderings. It is believed that St. John's Gospel was written originally in Greek, although the spoken language of Jesus was Aramaic and his scholarly language was Hebrew. The Greek word which has been variously translated "Counsellor" and "Comforter" is PARACLETOS. Because of the possibility of confusion as explained above it is not surprising that the copyists of the Greek text misspell the actual word used in the original which was PERICLYTOS. This means **The Admirable,** that is to say in Arabic: **Muhammad or Ahmed or Mahmoud.**

"And remember Jesus, the son of Mary, said: "O, children of Israel! I am the apostle of God sent to you confirming the Law which came before me, and giving glad tidings of an apostle to come after me, whose name shall be Ahmed."

Qur'ân 61:6

The Gospel of St. Matthew also reports Jesus prophesying the coming of Muhammad, the rejected Ishmaelite stone, and the rising of Muslim Ummah (nation) to whom the Kingdom of God shall be granted:

Jesus said to them, "Have you never read in the scriptures: "The very stone which the builders rejected has become the head of the corner; this was the Lord's doing, and it is marvelous in our eyes? Therefore I tell you, the kingdom of God will be taken away from you and given to a nation producing the fruits of it. And who falls on this stone will be broken to piece; but when it falls on any one, it will crush him." Matthew 21:42-44

Prophecy regarded the coming of the Prophet Muhammad is also found in the Old Testament. Moses is reported to be addressed by God in the following terms.

"I will raise up for them a prophet like you from among their <u>brethren</u>: And <u>I will put my words into his mouth,</u> and he shall speak to them all that I command him. And whoever will not give heed to my words which he shall speak in my name, I myself will require it of him. But the prophet who presumes to speak a word in my name which I have not commanded him to speak, or who speaks in the name of other gods, <u>that same prophet shall die.</u> And if you say in your heart, "How may we know the word which the Lord has not spoken?" When a prophet speaks

in the name of the Lord. If the word does not come to pass or come true that is a word which the Lord has not spoken; the prophet has spoken it presumptuously, you may not be afraid of him."   *Deuteronomy 18:18-22*

A prophet will be raised from among **"the brethren"** of the Israelites, and not from the Israelites themselves. The promised prophet must therefore come from among the Ishmaelites, i.e. the Arabs, who were the brethren of the Israelites. Abraham begot Ishmael and Isaac of the Jews.

"I will put my words into his mouth", says God. That is the exact description of the Holy Qur'ân, the only book which claims to be the direct speech of God. Muhammad was only God's mouthpiece, uttering the words as they were revealed to him directly, while faithful scribes put them down immediately as they were transmitted, and others memorized them for later transcription. God instructs him:

Say: "I am no bringer of a new-fangled doctrine among the apostles, nor do I know what will be done with me or with you. I follow that which is revealed to me by inspiration. I am but a Warner open and clear."   *Qur'ân 46:9*

The Qur'ân itself challenges those who entertain any doubt as to its divine authorship:

"If you are in doubt concerning this which We have revealed to Our servant then bring one chapter composed by man like this, and call your gods other than Allâh to witness if you speak the truth. And if you do not do it - and you will never do it - then fear the fire whose fuel is men and stones, kept ready for the unbelievers."
Qur'ân 2:23-24

For 1400 years that challenge has not yet been taken up by man or spirit. The Qur'ân is the standing miracle of Muhammad. It is not a miracle that is reported to have taken place, about which men could argue whether it really had happened or not. This is a miracle for eternity, a book inscribed.

a Guidance to mankind. You can read it today, tomorrow and forever. in its pure, unspoiled, inimitable Arabic as spoken by God Himself. You will be inspired by the grandeur of its style, by the wisdom and learning which it embodies, and by the loftiness of its moral and spiritual teachings.

My faith may be accused of influencing my assessment of the Qur'ân; so let the impartial pen of Edward Gibbon as a great historian, a distinguished men of letters, and an English Christian, be the judge. He writes:

"There is no book in the world in which God has been made such a theme of discourse as in the Holy Qur'ân.

It is impossible to conceive aught holier, nobler, purer, more sublime, more perfect, more supreme and more worthy of the Godhead than the God whom Muhammad worshipped. The ideal cannot be improved upon: one attribute taken from it would mar its perfection, and not one could be added to it would not be superfluous. Such is the lofty conception of Muhammad's God as presented in the Qur'ân. He has boldly had indelibly impressed the notion of the strictest monotheism upon the pages of history and towards this notion rational man cannot but drift surely if slowly."

It was this Book, then, which made the Muslims through their universities of Cordova, Cairo, Damascus and Baghdad, the founders of Algebra, Chemistry, Astronomy and Modern medicine at a time when Christian Europe was busily engaged in the futile controversies over Trinity, the Immaculate conception, salvation by blood and a god incarnate. To a man who knew not how to read or write, born in a community almost completely illiterate, the first verses ever to be revealed to him commanded:

"Read in the name of thy Lord who created - created man out of congealed blood; Read! and thy Lord is most bountiful, - He who taught by the pen, taught man that which he knew not." Qur'ân 96:1-5

Without this Book the learning of Greece, of Persia, of

India, of China and of Egypt, would forever have remained in the limbo of oblivion, instead of being preserved, enriched and bequeathed to the world of today. This was the Book that urged individual effort, the Book that made the seeking of knowledge a compulsory religious duty to every male and female. It is the Book that changed the sun, moon and the stars from being objects of worship to objects of study, subservient to man, as the Qur'ân rightly terms them. It is the Book that liberated the intellect of man, and widened his scope of enquiry into realms hitherto undreamt of.

"If you can pass beyond the zones of the heavens and the earth, pass! Not without authority will you be able to pass." Qur'ân 55:33

Before the incomparable symphony of its poetical prose and the profundity of its reason and logic which gushed forth from the illiterate Muhammad, the haughty eloquent Arabs of Hejaz stood aghast. They could only utter in amazed impotence: "This is nothing but magic!" Magic? from now on witchcraft, jugglery, exorcising of mentally sick persons from evil spirits and such petty stuff may be alright on an entertainment stage. This is the era of science and knowledge, and it is the uncorrupted and incorruptible Word of God spoken by God's holy servant as prophesied by Moses and Jesus, that ushers the new era. This and all nature around us are the standing miracles, the signs for those who ponder and mediate.

"Behold! In the creation of the heavens and the earth; in the alternation of the night and the day; in the sailing of the ships through the Ocean for the profit of mankind; in the rain which God sends down from the skies, and the life which He gives therewith to an earth that is dead; in the beasts of all kinds that he scatters through the earth; in the change of winds and the clouds which they trail like their slaves between the sky and the earth; (here) indeed are signs for a people that are wise." Qur'ân 2:164

"When a prophet speaks in the name of the Lord, if

the word does not come to pass or come true, that is a word which the Lord has not spoken; the prophet has spoken it presumptuously, you need not be afraid of him." That is what Moses was told by God about the prophet who was to come.

If Muhammad had any quality more pronounced than another it was the wonderful fulfillment of all what he foretold, whether as revealed to him in the form of the Qur'ân, or in his own capacity. It was a characteristic acknowledged and feared even by his enemies at his times. Of all the founders of religion his life is the least entangled in the cobwebs of legend. His foretelling of the victory of the Romans over the Persians, and that of the fledgeling little community of Muslims, hounded and oppressed, over the mighty super-powers of Rome and Persia, are but a few examples of the devastating exactitude of the fulfillment of his prophecies. All this while vehemently denying that he knew the future, being merely a Warner and a guide imparting God's message for the good of mankind. For indeed it was not he who spoke, but God the Knower-of-all-things who spoke through him.

"I wil raise for them a prophet like you," Moses is told. What was Moses like? A prophet who was also a political leader, an organizer of men, a legislator, a fugitive, who yet led his people out of oppression. Has there been in history any body like him, apart from Muhammad? Moses had the Torah, Muhammad the Qur'ân. Moses judged over the Israelites, Muhammad judged over the Muslim, Christian, Jew and Pagan. Moses led his people out of Egypt, Muhammad led his out of Mecca. The similarities are striking; the differences are mainly in degree.

"But the prophet who presumes to speak a word in my name which I have not commanded him to speak, or who speak in the name of other gods, that same prophet shall die." That divine threat is repeated in the Qur'ân:

"And if the apostle were to invent any sayings in Our

name, We should certainly seize him by his right hand, and we should certainly then cut off the artery of his heart; nor could any of you withhold him from our wrath."

Qur'ân 69:44-47

Death is the inevitable end of everyone born of woman. What is then the special meaning of God's statement to Moses that if a prophet was false he would "die"? Obviously it means meeting an untimely end or a violent death.

It is a historical fact that the Prophet Muhammad in spite of inhuman persecutions to which he was subjected, and the numerous attempts on his life, managed with God's help to escape every one of those attempts until finally he died peacefully on his bed at the ripe age of 63. It was after the completion of his mission which had taken him twenty three full years that he passed away to his maker. Three months before his death he could echo God's own words:

"Today I have completed and perfected for you your religion; and I have chosen for you Islam - Submission to the will of God - to be the religion." Six centuries before this Jesus said: *"My food is to do the will of him who sent me and to accomplish his work."*

They both met in Islam. (submission to the will of God) the religion that has no beginning and no end, for it is the religion of nature. God's own handiwork according to the pattern on which he has made mankind.

"So set thy face steadily to the faith, God's handiwork according to the pattern on which He has made mankind; there is no change in the work of God: that is the standard religion. But most men understand not." Qur'ân 30:30

To do the will of God is the eternal duty of man, and in this lies righteousness for this mortal life and salvation for the life to come which knows no mortality.

CONCLUSION

I started this essay with a quotation from Father John Mackenzie. I can do no better in concluding it that to quote from another Christian writer, Geoffrey Parrinder who wrote in his book: **Jesus in the Qur'ân:**

It is too easily assumed that all traditional doctrines are firmly based on the Bible. The Semitic view of God may need to be cleared of some Greek theories that overlaid it. Then if theology is to make contact with the modern world it must express itself in a meaningful way. Terms like Son of God, Trinity and Salvation need to be shaped and given new point. Concepts of prophecy, inspiration and revelation must be re-examined in view of the undoubted revelation of God in Muhammad and in the Qur'ân. Then much more real charity and generous understanding must be shown to members of other faiths. The example of Islam towards other people of the Book often puts us to shame. Christians always need to remember the words of Jesus, "Why call me, Lord, and do not do the things which I say?"

For more information about Islam, visit, write or call:

Islamic Da'wah & Guidance Center
Dammam, Postal Code 31131 - K.S.A.
Tel.: 8263535 - 8272772